Francis

With very best wishes, and thanks for the 'excellent

A Modest Little Man.

And perhaps we will collaborate on a project one day!

With best wishes
Mark Alva...

28th October 2022

Mayflower
They Knew They Were Pilgrims

by
Kate Glover

49Knights
Independent Publishing House,
Edinburgh & Cambridge

ISBN: 978-1-9993658-9-9

Please see page 6 for further copyright information.

Mayflower: They Knew They Were Pilgrims
by Kate Glover

*****

First Edition July 2022

First Printing

Foreword by John Valdimir Price

Text edited by Dan Lentell

Cover design by Paul Vine

Original portrait of the author by Susan Casanove

Typesetting by JT

*****

Further information about the play, licencing, as well
as current productions and tours can be found at
<u>admin@writersguild.org.uk</u>

Copyright Information

(See also page 4)

Video-recording
of amateur productions

Please note that the copyright laws governing video-recording are
extremely complex and that it should not be assumed that any play
may be video-recorded for whatever purpose without first obtaining
the permission of the appropriate agents. The fact that these plays
are published by 49Knights, Independent Publishing House,
Edinburgh & Cambridge, does not indicate that video rights are
available or that 49Knights controls such rights.

Foreword

The fourth definition of "pilgrim" in the *Oxford English Dictionary* cites the emigrants from England to America, designating them as the "Pilgrim Fathers." For any American of my generation, that is, someone born before or during the Second World War, the term was resonant with associations, historical, mythical, and social. No discourse, conversation, or argument could be conducted on the matter of the formation of what became the United States without these words and the pilgrims' search for religious freedom.

In 1802, almost two centuries after the arrival of the pilgrims and the establishment of the United States as a powerful and influential nation, John Quincy Adams (1767-1848), our sixth president and son of the second president John Adams (1735-1826) commended the pilgrims in these words: "Our affections as citizens embrace the whole extent of the Union ... and the names of Raleigh, Smith, Winthrop, Calvert, Penn, and Oglethorpe excite in our minds recollections equally pleasing and gratitude equally fervent with those of Carver and Bradford." To many Americans, I suspect these are just names now, though most of us could identify William Penn, who was, of course, a much later pilgrim.

In popular culture, we were frequently entertained and even enlightened by our Pilgrim Fathers for their passion and perseverance. The lyrics of Cole Porter's song, *Anything Goes* (1934), alluding to moral changes of the time, said of the pilgrims' landing on Plymouth rock in 1620 that today "Plymouth Rock would land on them." In the classic film, *The Man Who Shot Liberty Valance*, John Wayne refers, both affectionately and sarcastically, to the character played by James Stewart, as "Pilgrim," a "tenderfoot" or a person from the east coast unprepared for the ways and mores of the wild, wild west.

The first celebration of Thanksgiving on 11 November 1621 of the immigrant pilgrims with the Wampanoag Indians was a self-conscious assertion of the colonists' perception of themselves as pilgrims, very much like those mentioned in the prologue to Chaucer's *Canterbury*

Tales. The Pilgrim Fathers planned their departure from England's shores at the end of April 1620, about the same time of year as Chaucer's "folk" went on their pilgrimage to Canterbury. Alas, these English pilgrims had their voyage massively delayed, and while Canterbury was a pleasant but temporary destination, the Pilgrim fathers had permanent residence and religious freedom in mind.

Perhaps the most impressive achievement of the men on the Mayflower happened before they set foot on dry land, The *Mayflower Compact.* This document set forth some of the most basic principles by which the emigrants would be governed. They swore to plant a colony in Virginia, even though they were just off the coast of Massachusetts. They would "solemnly and mutually, in the Presence of God and one another, covenant and combine ourselves together into a civil Body Politick, for our better Ordering and Preservation, and Furtherance of the Ends aforesaid: And by Virtue hereof do enact, constitute, and frame, such just and equal Laws, Ordinances, Acts, Constitutions, and Offices, from time to time, as shall be thought most meet and convenient for the general Good of the Colony; unto which we promise all due Submission and Obedience." It was an ambitious programme, with far-reaching consequences and results.

- John Valdimir Price

Introduction

Historia Theatre Company specialises in putting on plays that have their source or inspiration in history. Over the last 25 years, we have tended to hone in on anniversaries and Mayflower is no exception. The play was written for performance in November 2020 to mark the 400th anniversary of the arrival of the Pilgrims off the coast of Massachusetts. Covid put a stop to our plans but we did manage a Zoom performance on November 22nd which was the exact date of the signing of the Mayflower Compact, a crucial document that looks forward to some of the principles enshrined in the Declaration of Independence. This was watched by an international audience, including many Americans. Last November as Covid was receding a little, we managed a modest tour of churches, most of which were the "doctrinal heirs " of the Pilgrims, professing many of their ideas. So, third time lucky we finally aim to put on a proper production, off book, in costume and enjoying the amenities of a proper theatre - The Hen And Chickens Theatre in Islington. This theatre also hosted Historia's first major production in June 1997.

The play portrays the trials and difficulties of the Pilgrims before they reached America. So, we focus on the determination of these men and women as they crossed the ocean from Plymouth, England to Plymouth Massachusetts, to worship in their own way.

We suffer with them as they faced huge odds: bullying by the venture capitalists of the day, sickness and death on board, leaking ships, terrifying storms at sea, and personal heartbreak... And we try to discover what they would find when they got there.

- **Kate Glover**
- Author, *Mayflower: They New They Were Pilgrims*

Mayflower: They Knew They Were Pilgrims

The first preview of the play took place, for COVID reasons, on 22 November 2020 as a Zoom event watched by an international audience. There followed a short script in hand tour around London churches in November 2021. A full production opened at The Hen And Chickens Theatre, London and ran from 24 May until 11 June 2022.

Written by Kate Glover

Directed by Kenneth Michaels

Sound design by Michael Murray

Set design by Eliza Podesta

Lighting design by Edmund Sutton

The play lasts approximately 120 mins

Cast for STAGED PREMIERE 24 th MAY-11 th JUNE 2022

Edward Winslow	- *Simon Brandon*
Mrs Magdalen Winslow	- *Kate Glover*
Pastor John Robinson	- *Stephen Riddle*
William Brewster	- *Kenneth Michaela*
Elizabeth Winslow	- *Francesca Baker*
William Bradford	- *Daniel Chrisostomou*
Thomas Weston	- *Harry Saks*
Dorothy Bradford	- *Emily Harry*
Captain Christopher Jones	- *Kenneth Michaels*
Christopher Martin	- *Harry Saks*
Stephen Hopkins	- *Stephen Riddle*
John Billington	- *Simon Brandon*
Mrs Mary Brewster	- *Kate Glover*
Thomas Henley	- *Harry Saks*

We were grateful to James Price, Emma Riches and Maeve Brennan for covering the roles of William and Dorothy Bradford.

* * * * *

Casts for NOVEMBER 2020 and NOVEMBER 2021 included:

Elizabeth Winslow	- *Georgia Riley*
Dorothy Bradford	- *Laetitia Coulson & Clare Langford*
William Bradford	- *James Price*
Pastor Robinson / Stephen Hopkins	- *Robin Marchal*
John Billington	- *Michael Murray*

* * * * *

Notes on the text: SFX = sound and/or lighting effect.

The minor roles of CLERK to Thomas Weston and CREW are played by members of the cast.

CHARACTERS IN ORDER OF APPEARANCE

Edward Winslow: *Religious but not obsessively so. Gets on well with people. Enthusiastic and charming. Supportive and practical. Gifted linguist (learns one of the Indian languages). Originally from Worcester.*

Mrs Magdalen Winslow: *Edward's mother. Adores her son but cannot understand why his religion is forcing him to flee the country.*

Pastor John Robinson: *Tall and dark. Distinguished Protestant theologian who had to resign his post at Corpus Christi College Cambridge because of his dissenting views. Minister to the exiled Separatist congregation in Leiden, which meets in his house at Groenepointe on the Kloksteeg in Leiden. Devoted to the needs of his followers. Charismatic and much loved.*

William Brewster: *Former diplomat, forced to resign because of his religious views. Hid John Robinson in his house in Scrooby Manor. Escaped with Robinson and the Scrooby congregation to Leiden in 1609. Once in Leiden, ran the Brewster Press, publishing Puritan literature.*

Elizabeth Winslow: *Spirited wife of Edward. Intelligent and assertive*

William Bradford: *Intense and driven. A natural leader. From 1621 was the governor of the Plymouth colony until his death in 1657.*

Thomas Weston: *Dodgy businessman, acting for the Merchant Adventurers, the venture capitalists of their day.*

Dorothy Bradford: *Beautiful and petite but emotionally fragile. Daughter of English couple living in Leiden.*

Captain Christopher Jones: *Captain of the Mayflower which he part owns. Originally from Harwich, now living in Southwark, he is an experienced and skilled seaman and navigator - fortunately for the Pilgrims.*

Christopher Martin: *Bullying and dishonest man appointed by the Merchant Adventurers to procure supplies for the voyage. Refused to co-operate with anyone else. Was extremely unpleasant to crew and passengers on the Mayflower.*

Stephen Hopkins: *One of the so-called 'Strangers' who joined the Pilgrims at Southampton. The only one who had any proper experience of the New World. He lived in Jamestown for 5 years and survived shipwreck off Bermuda in 1609. Assertive and confident.*

John Billington: *Somewhat disreputable and 'wild'; character, father of uncontrollable sons. Another of the 'Strangers'. Was the first person to be executed for murder in the Plymouth colony.*

Mary Brewster: *Supportive wife of William Brewster.*

Thomas Henley: *Unpleasant, jeering sailor who taunts the Pilgrims while onboard ship.*

ACT 1: Scene 1

[The house of Edward WINSLOW London 1617. WINSLOW and his mother, MAGDALEN, are seated.]

MAGDALEN: I don't understand you, Edward. You are throwing away a wonderful opportunity of employment. You are ruining your life.

WINSLOW: No Mother, you don't understand

MAGDALEN: I'm afraid I do. You are halfway through your eight-year apprenticeship. You could become a Master of the Printers Guild. Profitable employment for life.

WINSLOW: Mother ...

MAGDALEN: I do know what I'm talking about. Your father and I were married at St Bride's remember?

WINSLOW: What's that got to do with anything?

MAGDALEN: The Printers' Church. We knew so many printers. We understand the trade. You need to finish your apprenticeship.

WINSLOW: Mother, if you would let me speak.

MAGDALEN: Very well.

WINSLOW: I have employment.

MAGDALEN: You can't have. You haven't finished your training.

WINSLOW: It's in Leiden, Holland

MAGDALEN: Oh. Abroad.

WINSLOW: You don't have to take that tone Mother.

MAGDALEN: English printers are the best in the world.

WINSLOW: But I will be working for an English printer. In
                Leiden.

MAGDALEN: A bit of a backwater no doubt. Couldn't you
                have managed Amsterdam?

WINSLOW: Leiden is much more interesting than
                Amsterdam.

MAGDALEN: How do you know? You've never been there.

WINSLOW: It has a very famous university. And a lot of
                English people are living there

MAGDALEN: But why? Why do you need to take some half
                baked job - and abroad at that - when your
                career is all mapped out for you here?

WINSLOW: That's just it Mother. It is not mapped out. I
                don't fit in.

MAGDALEN: You have always fitted in. At school, at church.
                You have lots of friends

WINSLOW: I can't go to Church here Mother.

MAGDALEN: What are you talking about?

WINSLOW: I can no longer take the Eucharist in the
                Church of England. I just can't. The church
                here has grown alien to me.

MAGDALEN: I had no idea you felt like that. *[Pause.]* You never said anything before.

WINSLOW: I don't think I knew myself. It has sort of crept up on me while I have been here in London. And now I am convinced there is no going back.

MAGDALEN: Well you had better not tell your sister that. She is about to marry ...

WINSLOW: A clergyman. Yes, I know and I wish Magdalen every happiness.

MAGDALEN: It's a very good match I'll have you know. William Wake is gentry. From Dorset.

WINSLOW: Yes mother.

MAGDALEN: She's done well. And now you seek to spoil everything by having these hare-brained ideas about the church.

WINSLOW: I have no intention of ruining Magdalen's happiness Mother but I have been reading a lot and thinking. The Church of England has changed. I can't take all this kneeling down, exchanging of rings, crossing myself at the name of Jesus, all the ceremonial.

MAGDALEN: But it's beautiful. The beauty of holiness. The organ, the hymns, the stained glass windows, the processions.

WINSLOW: It reeks of popery mother. And they don't even respect the Bible

MAGDALEN: We have lessons from the Bible every week. What are you talking about?

WINSLOW: Mother, there are no bishops in the Bible.

MAGDALEN: This is the seventeenth century after Christ.
                Things have changed since His day. So, we
                need bishops now.

WINSLOW: We do not. The church must be organised and
                governed by the people. We need preachers
                who expound on the Scriptures. But that's it.
                We don't need bishops more preoccupied with
                status and vestments than with true religion.

MAGDALEN: You are beginning to sound suspiciously
                like a Puritan. I hope very much you are not
                beginning to associate with these kinds of
                people. You know what happened in Hereford?

WINSLOW: What?

MAGDALEN: The Rev'd William Hoskins made no secret of
                his Puritan views. So, they hauled him before
                the Courts of High Commission. He was
                excommunicated and declared unfit to lead his
                parish.

WINSLOW: I remember William. I am sorry to hear it.

MAGDALEN: So are his family. Five children. How do you
                think he is going to look after them? Such a
                nice little church too. Just outside Ledbury.
                [*Pause.*] I forget the name.

WINSLOW: I think I know where you mean. I'm sorry it's
                happened to him but it's happening to lots of
                others and this is why I have to go.

MAGDALEN: But you are not a clergyman.

WINSLOW: I have views that the Church can't agree with. And if I make them public, I am risking excommunication, imprisonment, or even death.

MAGDALEN: They wouldn't execute you, surely. Not just for a few little views about kneeling.

WINSLOW: Mother, I work for John Beale. He publishes Puritan tracts and he imports similar works from Holland. His colleagues are being watched all the time. One of them has been arrested several times. I can't wait any longer. I have to go. Can't you see that?

MAGDALEN: But can't you be a little more diplomatic about the way you express your views?

WINSLOW: How can I be "diplomatic" about something so important?

MAGDALEN: I'll miss you terribly. You know that. And so will all your brothers and sisters. We have hardly seen you since you've been in London.

WINSLOW: I know. I've been busy. And travel to Worcester is not easy these days.

MAGDALEN: I know that my darling.

WINSLOW: Mother! [*Hugs her.*]

MAGDALEN: I love you so much, Edward. And I can't bear to lose you - and in a foreign country too.

WINSLOW: I love you too Mother. [*Pause.*] I never intended this. I didn't set out to alienate myself from you and the family.

MAGDALEN: I know you didn't. You've always been such
             a good son. *[Pause.]* It's almost as though you
             have had a sort of conversion?

WINSLOW: Perhaps. All I know is that I can't lie about how
             I feel.

MAGDALEN: I see. You were always like that. [Pause.] When
             are you thinking of going?

WINSLOW: [Pause.] Next week.

MAGDALEN: What?

WINSLOW: I have no choice.

MAGDALEN: You'll miss your sister's wedding.

WINSLOW: I'll write to Magdalen.

MAGDALEN: Where will you live?

WINSLOW: William Brewster said he would find something
             for me.

MAGDALEN: Who?

WINSLOW: William Brewster. He was part of a separatist
             church in Scrooby near Nottingham. They
             used to meet in a private room, but then they
             were betrayed. So, they had to escape.

MAGDALEN: All this cloak and dagger business is beyond
             me. Why can't you just accept the articles of
             the Church of England? Lots of people have
             reservations, but they just get on with life.

WINSLOW: Well, I think that's dishonest.

MAGDALEN: *[Wearily.]* You would.

WINSLOW: Anyway, Brewster has been in Leiden for nearly ten years now and he runs a printing press. Among other things.

MAGDALEN: What sort of printing press?

WINSLOW: You wouldn't like it mother. They publish religious books for sale in England - but not the kind of books you would approve of.

MAGDALEN: I see

WINSLOW: The sale of these books is forbidden in England. They are not exactly complementary to the Church of England.

MAGDALEN: Oh Edward. Why do you have to get involved in these things?

WINSLOW: Mother, it does mean I have work, and Mr Brewster says I can have a room in his house.

MAGDALEN: Have you met him?

WINSLOW: No, but I have heard good things about him.

MAGDALEN: Well. It seems you have made up your mind.

WINSLOW: Exactly.

MAGDALEN: There's nothing more I can do darling son except pray for you.

WINSLOW: Mother...

MAGDALEN: Write to me. *[Emotional.]* I must leave. You have
                 things to do. The family are waiting for me at
                 Careswell.

WINSLOW: *[Hugs her.]* Oh, give my love to the old house.

MAGDALEN: I will. The house is not the same without you.

WINSLOW: I will see you again Mother.

MAGDALEN: Godspeed my son. My lovely son.

[Exeunt.]

ACT 1: Scene 2

[Leiden, Groenepointe on the Kloksteeg. 1619. The weekly service is finishing. The people are singing, unaccompanied, the first verses of Psalm 107. The cast take turns singing verses 1-11.]

{01}   Give thanks unto the Lord, for he is gracious: and his mercy endureth for ever.

{02}   Let them give thanks whom the Lord hath redeemed: and delivered from the hand of the enemy;

{03}   And gathered them out of the lands, from the east, and from the west: from the north, and from the south.

{04}   They went astray in the wilderness out of the way: and found no city to dwell in;

{05}   Hungry and thirsty: their soul fainted in them.

{06}   So they cried unto the Lord in their trouble: and he delivered them from their distress.

{07}   He led them forth by the right way: that they might go to the city where they dwelt.

{08}   O that men would therefore praise the Lord for his goodness: and declare the wonders that he doeth for the children of men!

{09}   For he satisfieth the empty soul: and filleth the hungry soul with goodness.

{10}   Such as sit in darkness, and in the shadow of death: being fast bound in misery and iron;

{11}   Because they rebelled against the words of the Lord: and lightly regarded the counsel of the most High.

ROBINSON: Be of good cheer brethren. Pass the week
                 in faith and in determination to live by the
                 scriptures and the word of Our Lord.

ALL: Amen.

*[All exeunt except EDWARD Winslow, John ROBINSON and William
BREWSTER.]*

ROBINSON: William Brewster and Edward Winslow. My
                 friends. What is it?

BREWSTER: We're in trouble.

ROBINSON: I can see that. What's happened?

WINSLOW: Elder Brewster and I decided to publish Perth
                 Assembly

BREWSTER: I will not have you taking the blame on yourself
                 Edward. It was my decision to publish.

ROBINSON: Perth Assembly? It's an inflammatory book. In
                 fact, it's the most contentious in years.

BREWSTER: We hear from our people in England that King
                 James is furious.

ROBINSON: Well yes he would be. Are you really surprised?

WINSLOW: We didn't think they would find out so quickly.

ROBINSON: King James cannot conceive of any religion
                 without bishops. And this book attacks the
                 imposition of bishops on Scotland.

BREWSTER: Well, we cannot conceive of any role that
                 bishops might fill - in any true religion.

ROBINSON: But you published here in Leiden. How has the news got back to England?

BREWSTER: We smuggled the book to Scotland in wine vats and ...

ROBINSON: In what?

WINSLOW: Wine vats, Pastor Robinson.

ROBINSON: Well... I cannot accuse you of lacking imagination.

WINSLOW: Was it wrong?

ROBINSON: The timing is not ideal.

BREWSTER: Meaning?

ROBINSON: The impact on our plans for getting to America could be damaging.

BREWSTER: How so?

ROBINSON: We need money. We are in the middle of negotiations.

BREWSTER: God will provide.

ROBINSON: We need a ship, we need equipment. We need money to pay the sailors. It's a lot to ask God...

WINSLOW: I thought John Carver had been negotiating about monies with the Virginia Company.

ROBINSON: He was doing very well and also had hopes of getting a patent to settle in Virginia via his contacts with the Privy Council. But now ...

WINSLOW: They might not appreciate our little publication.

ROBINSON: The reputation of the Leiden congregation could certainly be tarnished in their eyes. This could put the negotiations at risk.

WINSLOW: *[Notices someone offstage.]* Elizabeth!

[ELIZABETH Winslow, Edward's new wife, rushes in, panting.]

ELIZABETH: Excuse me for disturbing you all but...

ROBINSON: Sit down. Catch your breath. What's happened?

ELIZABETH: I walked back past the printing press after service and there were soldiers ...

WINSLOW: Soldiers?

ELIZABETH: They had burst in. They were just smashing the type and the presses with their weapons. It's chaos.

BREWSTER: How many were there?

ELIZABETH: At least twenty. You must come and see. Perhaps you can stop them.

BREWSTER: We must go Pastor Robinson.

[Exeunt.]

ACT 1: Scene 3

[Leiden: Groenepointe on the Kloksteeg. 1619. One hour later. John ROBINSON is reading a theological book. ELIZABETH knocks and enters.]

ELIZABETH: Can I talk to you, Pastor Robinson? There are certain questions in my heart that I cannot resolve. I have tried prayer but I don't seem to be getting very far. *[Pause.]*

ELIZABETH: Forgive me, Pastor Robinson. I am disturbing you.

ROBINSON: Not at all Mistress Winslow. Will you sit down?

ELIZABETH: Thank you.

ROBINSON: What is the news at the Press?

ELIZABETH: Worse than we feared. They have damaged all the presses. All the type has been smashed. The windows have been broken and they have locked the doors.

ROBINSON: So you couldn't even get in?

ELIZABETH: No. All we could do was to peer through the windows. Glass everywhere. One of the soldiers told us it had been locked on the orders of the town council. But then there was another rumour that the soldiers were in the pay of the English ambassador here.

ROBINSON: Interesting. Did you hear the soldiers speak?

ELIZABETH: I think they were English. But maybe some
               were Dutch. They tore up the manuscripts
               too. There was one book that Elder Brewster
               had almost finished printing, and the soldiers
               poured water on it - along with a whole pile of
               dung. And we just can't get in.

ROBINSON: How is Elder Brewster?

ELIZABETH: Very shocked and very upset.

ROBINSON: His life is in danger. He needs to flee.

ELIZABETH: That is what Edward told him.

ROBINSON: Edward has a shrewd head on his shoulders.

ELIZABETH: There is a Dutch family in a village near Breda.
               Very remote. Elder Brewster met them while he
               was a diplomat. He can go there for a while.
               And then maybe he will have to take the family
               to England and hide out there.

ROBINSON: Not easy with a big family.

ELIZABETH: No. *[Pause.]* Do you think Edward is safe?

ROBINSON: Apart from the fact he has lost his position, he
               is in far less danger than Brewster. He was a
               hired hand. But he needs to be discreet.

ELIZABETH: Yes.

ROBINSON: You said you had something to tell me.

ELIZABETH: Yes. I am not sure how to put this, but it
               concerns the plans for the New World.

ROBINSON: You don't want to go?

ELIZABETH: *[Taken aback.]* How did you know? Is it that obvious?

ROBINSON: For those who have eyes to see ... *[Gently.]* Why not Elizabeth?

ELIZABETH: I don't see the point - at least not for me and Edward.

ROBINSON: Have you told Edward this ?

ELIZABETH: Not in so many words, but I think he might suspect.

ROBINSON: You need to tell him. He is very enthusiastic about going.

ELIZABETH: I know.

ROBINSON: I ask you again. Why don't you want to go?

ELIZABETH: I think it is mad. We are able to worship in the way we wish here in Leiden. We are not at risk of being excommunicated or executed - unless we draw attention to ourselves as Elder Brewster and Edward have done. We have no idea what awaits us there - probably nothing at all. Just vast expanses of nothingness. And that would be the best we could expect. At worst, we would be pursued and killed by savage tribes who feel that we are taking away land that isn't ours. I think we should give thanks for the freedom of worship we have here and just stop drawing attention to ourselves.

ROBINSON: You have heard the arguments in favour of going?

ELIZABETH: Yes. And some of them, if you will excuse me,
                Pastor, are ridiculous. Some families think
                their children are becoming too "Dutch"! The
                children are learning Dutch - as they should.
                They have Dutch friends - which is natural.

ROBINSON: These are good points. But you must agree that
                life here is hard. The Dutch employers are hard
                taskmasters.

ELIZABETH: Yes, I know that. And I know that many people
                are being forced to do jobs well below their
                qualifications. I was shocked to find out that
                Elder Brewster used to be a diplomat, and now
                he is merely a printer. But I believe, Pastor
                Robinson, that things will improve. When the
                Dutch masters see what good employees we are,
                and how hard we work - especially in the wool
                industry, our conditions will get better.

ROBINSON: It is possible you are being slightly over-
                optimistic here!

ELIZABETH: Well even if things don't get easier, it is
                certainly a lot better than going out to some
                barren inhospitable continent.

ROBINSON: The other problem, and I think you are aware
                of this, is that there has recently been a treaty
                between the English and the Dutch.

ELIZABETH: I didn't know. I don't take much interest in
                international politics.

ROBINSON: Perhaps you should. The Dutch need the
                support of the English in their war against
                Spain.

ELIZABETH: Will this affect us?

ROBINSON: Of course, it will. In return for the support of King James, the Dutch have promised not to allow the printing of any more books which may be deemed offensive to the English.

ELIZABETH: But that was what the Brewster Press was doing. So even if they can get it repaired...

ROBINSON: Precisely. That's the end of it. No more work.

ELIZABETH: Such a shame. They were putting out good books.

ROBINSON: And, even more damaging, the Dutch have undertaken not to support any more independent English religious congregations.

ELIZABETH: Like us?

ROBINSON: Yes. Like us.

ELIZABETH: But we can stay the way we are?

ROBINSON: For the moment, yes, but we have to behave ourselves.

ELIZABETH: I see.

ROBINSON: But there is another reason for going to America that we haven't talked about. I think you know what it is Elizabeth.

ELIZABETH: "We go as Pilgrims"? That argument?

ROBINSON: Exactly. We know we are pilgrims. It is part of our Covenant with God. To spread the Gospel.

ELIZABETH: But how do we know ...?

ROBINSON: Just a moment. Listen to this. *[Reads.]* "You
                  shall have made this island, which is but as the
                  suburbs of the old world, a bridge, a gallery
                  to the new, to join all to that world that shall
                  never grow old, the kingdom of heaven."

ELIZABETH: Is that just a fancy way of saying that it would
                  be a good idea to try to convert the Indians - if
                  they happen to be around?

ROBINSON: *[Laughs.]* You are refreshingly irreverent
                  Mistress Winslow! But yes, I think that is what
                  John Donne has in mind.

ELIZABETH: John Donne! Forgive me. My parents have
                  often chided me about speaking before I think.

ROBINSON: I like your candour Mistress Winslow. *[Pause.]*
                  We are a very long way from orchestrating a
                  move to America. And the fact that William
                  Brewster is being forced to go into hiding will
                  slow things up, perhaps for some years. But
                  imagine that our negotiations are successful,
                  that we are able to secure a patent to establish a
                  settlement in the New World, what would you
                  do? Your husband is very enthusiastic about a
                  move. Are you minded to stay behind in Leiden
                  if he decides to go to America?

ELIZABETH: I can't imagine him leaving me here.

ROBINSON: Would you stop him leaving?

ELIZABETH: We haven't talked about it Pastor Robinson.
                  We married in haste. We didn't know each
                  other well.

ROBINSON: I understand.

ELIZABETH: I'm not the only person to have doubts. Dorothy Bradford, William's wife, is in agony because they think they might have to leave their little baby son behind. And she can't bear to think of it.

ROBINSON: But their problem is not your problem. Perhaps you need to talk to Edward?

ELIZABETH: I'll try. *[Rises.]* Thank you for listening Pastor Robinson.

ROBINSON: Good Luck - and thank you for your honesty!

ELIZABETH: Goodbye.

[ELIZABETH exits.]

ROBINSON: O God the teacher of us all. Have mercy upon thy little flock here in Leiden. Give wisdom to us all as we discuss our next moves. And help us to fulfil our part of the Covenant that we have with Thee. Forgive me for my low spirits. Forgive me for doubting that our dreams may ever materialise. Forgive me for focusing on the things of Mammon like money when instead we should be looking to establish thy Kingdom in foreign climes. But alas my God, I have doubts. Grave doubts. Forgive me Lord, for I am a sinner.

[ROBINSON bows his head and exits.]

ACT 1: Scene 4

[The house of ELIZABETH and Edward WINSLOW. 1619. Two weeks later.]

WINSLOW: So you confided in Pastor Robinson before mentioning anything to me. How do you think that makes me look?

ELIZABETH: I just didn't know how to broach the subject with you. You are so keen to leave. I just didn't want to deflate you.

WINSLOW: But why, Elizabeth. Why?

ELIZABETH: We haven't got any capital. Nothing is organised. Crossing the Atlantic is dangerous.

WINSLOW: You've never been a coward.

ELIZABETH: It never occurred to me that we might all die until we heard about that group of English separatists who tried to get to Virginia from what's it called - that city in Germany, you know where I mean, just over the border - Emden.

WINSLOW: That was terrible.

ELIZABETH: More than terrible. The numbers involved were heartbreaking. Something like a hundred and eighty of them left, and a hundred and thirty died. Three-quarters of them. I heard they were packed together like herrings and there was no fresh water.

WINSLOW: Well, that boiled down to immoral practice by the financiers, I'm afraid. They wanted to get as much money as possible and so they packed far too many people into the ship.

ELIZABETH: And you think that won't happen to us?

WINSLOW: It is just a question of careful negotiation Elizabeth. And we have to make sure that the people who sponsor us are trustworthy.

ELIZABETH: With William Brewster still in hiding, no-one knows what to do. We're just leaderless without him. And ...

WINSLOW: I know what you're going to say - that no-one wants to invest in the Separatists from Leiden anymore; we are almost tainted.

ELIZABETH: Exactly. After you and Brewster decided to publish that book. I still don't understand what got into you.

WINSLOW: It was a question of principle. Brewster decided it would be moral cowardice not to publish. We don't believe in the necessity of bishops so why shrink from a book like Perth Assembly that makes that point clear?

ELIZABETH: Because we also need money to get to Virginia - or wherever it is we're going. Publishing that stupid - and not brilliantly written - book was tantamount to abandoning all our plans to leave Leiden. One doesn't bite the hand of the one who feeds us.

WINSLOW: Calm down. All this shouting will not help.

ELIZABETH: [Shouting.] I am not shouting.

WINSLOW: Well, whatever you want to call it. Please Elizabeth.

[They sit.]

ELIZABETH: I'm not the only person who feels like that.
                    Look at Dorothy Bradford.

WINSLOW: That's different.

ELIZABETH: How's it different?

WINSLOW: They have a child.

ELIZABETH: Well we might have a child.

WINSLOW: Elizabeth, are you ...?

ELIZABETH: Not yet, but you never know. Anyway ...

[Loud knocking at the door. William BRADFORD enters.]

WINSLOW: William Bradford! We were just talking about
                    you and Dorothy.

BRADFORD: Oh?

ELIZABETH: *[Quickly.]* Dorothy was telling me that baby John
                    had just turned two! Hardly a baby anymore!

BRADFORD: He's a funny little creature. Good at making us
                    laugh. But forgive me for bursting in like this. I
                    have news.

WINSLOW: Oh, please tell us.

BRADFORD: It concerns the negotiations. I think there has
                    been a breakthrough. I had a letter from Robert
                    Cushman in London. He's made contact
                    with a business associate of the Merchant
                    Adventurers; a man called Thomas Weston.

ELIZABETH: Merchant Adventurers? You mean "investors"?

BRADFORD: Yes, if you prefer. Weston has managed to obtain a patent from the Privy Council to establish a settlement in the New World. He's had the idea of forming a sort of joint-stock company...

ELIZABETH: How would it work?

BRADFORD: The details still have to be worked out.

ELIZABETH: I thought as much.

WINSLOW: Elizabeth!

ELIZABETH: Sorry, I'm being hasty.

BRADFORD: In fact, we do know quite a lot, courtesy of Robert Cushman. We had to keep the name of the Leiden congregation out of the negotiations because of that publication of Perth Assembly.

WINSLOW: Yes.

BRADFORD: The tide of opinion is turning in England. King James is getting his way and they're calling us irresponsible fanatics.

ELIZABETH: So what's the solution? How do we get financial backing?

BRADFORD: Thomas Weston has persuaded the Privy Council to grant him a patent in his name to start up a private plantation. As for the Separatists from Leiden - we are not even mentioned in that document!

WINSLOW: Is he going to finance it all himself? What's in it for him?

BRADFORD: He's cleverer than that. He has persuaded
                 several Merchant Adventurers to put up most
                 of the capital.

WINSLOW: But how?

BRADFORD: He's convinced that he can make money from
                 the fishing - and the fur trade. So of course, the
                 investors would benefit.

ELIZABETH: Well that's a point I suppose. People can make
                 a lot of money from the fur trade.

BRADFORD: And this is where you two come in

WINSLOW: Us?

BRADFORD: You were thinking of making a quick visit
                 to England, weren't you? Something about
                 Elizabeth's inheritance?

ELIZABETH: My stepmother, in Suffolk, has just died and it
                 seems I am her heir.

WINSLOW: So we need to go to England and see through
                 the sale of Elizabeth's property.

BRADFORD: When do you go?

WINSLOW: Not sure. Sooner rather than later.

ELIZABETH: Why?

BRADFORD: Cushman needs a bit of help dealing with
                 Thomas Weston. William Brewster is in hiding
                 and I can't leave Leiden for the moment either.

WINSLOW: Oh?

BRADFORD: I have a buyer for the little house I bought here.
             A sale is imminent. I need to see it through.
             And we need the money for the voyage.

ELIZABETH: So you want us to meet up with this Thomas
             Weston and see if he is genuine?

BRADFORD: In a nutshell, yes. Robert Cushman is not a
             well man. I just think that more of us need to
             have met Mr Weston. So much depends on
             him. He has promised to find a ship for us too.
             Plus the captain and crew.

WINSLOW: I think we can do that. What do you feel
             Elizabeth?

ELIZABETH: Yes indeed. We'll meet him and tell you what
             we think.

BRADFORD: That's wonderful and I think it will speed
             things up too. *[Pause.]* Dorothy is not happy
             about any of this you know.

ELIZABETH: I had wondered.

BRADFORD: I think baby John will be too young to sail.
             We'll have to leave him here.

ELIZABETH: No!

BRADFORD: Better that than him dying on the voyage. But
             Dorothy won't even discuss it. So I just can't
             leave her either.

WINSLOW: I feel for you, my friend. *[Pause.]* We'll do our
             best with the mysterious Mr Weston!

BRADFORD: I can't thank you enough. Godspeed.

[Exeunt.]

ACT 1: Scene 5

[England early 1620. The office of Thomas WESTON in London. We hear horses and carriages and the sounds of the City. WESTON is at his desk with a sheaf of papers. We hear a knock on the door.]

WESTON: Come.

[Enter ELIZABETH and Edward WINSLOW. WESTON rises.]

WESTON: Thomas Weston. Delighted to meet you.

WINSLOW: Edward Winslow. And this is my wife Elizabeth.

WESTON: Enchanted!

[Shaking both their hands vigorously; a little too touchy-feely with ELIZABETH. She doesn't like this.]

                   So your business in Suffolk has been
                   satisfactorily concluded Mrs Winslow?

ELIZABETH: *[Coldly.]* Yes thank you.

WESTON: Do sit. And when do we expect to see Mr
                   Robert Cushman?

WINSLOW: Mr Cushman is unwell and he sends apologies.
                   He says he has the most excruciating pains in
                   his chest. A bundle of lead as it were, crushing
                   his heart. That's how he describes it.

WESTON: Most unpleasant.

WINSLOW: Indeed. But we have seen him, and he has
                   briefed us. It is very good to meet you especially
                   as you yourself are in sympathy with our goals.

WESTON: Indeed I am. Your determination to worship
            in your own way - even at your peril - strikes
            me as extremely praiseworthy. And then your
            ambitions to plant religion in the New World.
            I am in awe of you Mr Winslow. I am not sure
            I would quite have the moral courage that you
            all seem to possess.

WINSLOW: But you have skills and contacts Mr Weston
            that we all admire. I think you have news for
            us?

WESTON: I have met with a group of Merchant
            Adventurers. Our strategy is to form a joint-
            stock company which means that each of you
            - "Pilgrims" shall I say - will be given a share in
            the company, worth ten pounds.

WINSLOW: Ten pounds! That's very generous

WESTON: Yes but in a sense, you have to earn it Mr
            Winslow! The Merchant Adventurers expect
            that once you are in America, you will be able
            to generate profit through cod fishing and the
            fur trade.

ELIZABETH: So you will then help yourselves to those
            profits?

WESTON: Well that's a slightly blunt version of what
            actually happens, my dear Mrs Winslow! The
            idea is that for the next seven years, the Pilgrims
            will work six days a week...

WINSLOW: As we do now?

WESTON: And of those six days, you work four for the
            Merchant Adventurers and two for yourselves.

WINSLOW: Ingenious!

WESTON: And at the end of the seven years, we divide the
               capital and profits among everyone. So, if all has
               gone to plan, the Pilgrims, by this arrangement,
               will own their own homes along with the land
               that goes with them, free of any obligation to
               the Company of Merchant Adventurers. You
               will own your own homes absolutely.

ELIZABETH: It almost sounds too good to be true!

WINSLOW: Elizabeth!

WESTON: Have faith my dear Mrs Winslow. Have faith.
               There is such abundance of fur and fish in the
               New World that this plan cannot fail.

WINSLOW: It is an excellent plan Mr Weston. Hearty
               congratulations and grateful thanks are in
               order, I think.

WESTON: You are very kind Mr Winslow. Now, I would
               like you to look at some documents in which
               the arrangements are set out and then we can
               begin to set all this in motion.

WINSLOW: And the ship?

WESTON: I have many contacts among the shipping
               community. We will get you a ship, fully fitted
               out, with a captain and crew.

ELIZABETH: And properly seaworthy?

WESTON: Oh yes, it will be properly checked over.

WINSLOW: You heard about the people who tried to sail
               from Emden?

WESTON: Indeed, I did. A bad business, a very bad business. Tragic. We have been trying to find out about the people who were behind that.

ELIZABETH: I'm very glad to hear that.

WESTON: Now, do excuse me while I fetch the copies of the documents. My clerk has been working on this all morning.

[WESTON exits.]

WINSLOW: Things are beginning to look much more promising.

ELIZABETH: If you can believe what he says.

WINSLOW: Elizabeth, I really don't see what can go wrong.

ELIZABETH: Well I didn't like the way he stared at me for a start.

WINSLOW: I didn't either. But just because he likes pretty young women doesn't mean he can't do business.

ELIZABETH: And I didn't believe all those fine words about having sympathy with our aims to plant religion in the New World. Just words.

WINSLOW: He was trying to be nice.

ELIZABETH: I am sorry to seem so negative my love, but there is something about him I just don't trust. And I can't put my finger on it. I just don't think we have met the real Thomas Weston yet.

[Sound of raised voices outside.]

CLERK: It's a really long document, Mr Weston.

WESTON: That's no excuse Evans. Just get it finished
                  within the hour. I have clients here.

WINSLOW: Well he's all we've got. We have to trust him.
                  Shh. He's coming back

[Enter WESTON.]

WESTON: I'm afraid my clerk has been very dilatory. He
                  arrived late this morning, and hasn't finished
                  copying all the documents yet. Please accept my
                  apologies.

WINSLOW: Of course.

WESTON: Well the only thing to do while we wait is to
                  dine. Allow me to take you to an excellent
                  tavern.

WINSLOW: Thank you. We accept with pleasure. Elizabeth?

WESTON: After you Mrs Winslow.

[Exeunt.]

ACT 1: Scene 6

[The Winslows' Home May 1620. ROBINSON and BRADFORD are sitting with ELIZABETH Winslow.]

ROBINSON: So, no-one has heard from William Brewster?

BRADFORD: He's lying low. I suppose he thinks he will put us in danger if he contacts any of us.

ROBINSON: And still nothing from Thomas Weston?

BRADFORD: Nothing.

ELIZABETH: He was supposed to be organising a ship for us. It was all part of the deal. It was actually there in black and white in the papers we saw.

BRADFORD: There's nothing for it. We're going to have to get one ourselves.

ROBINSON: William Bradford I admire your energy and determination, but none of us has any knowledge of ships.

BRADFORD: Actually I have talked to a number of people from the Congregation. There are a few men who have worked in shipping and could help us make the choice. They have real expertise.

ROBINSON: But what about money? That could be the sticking point.

BRADFORD: I have succeeded in selling my little house. And so have many others. We are ready to pledge that money for the voyage.

ELIZABETH: Ah, here's Edward.

[Enter Edward WINSLOW.]

WINSLOW:	I have some news.
ELIZABETH:	Not good by the look of you.
WINSLOW:	I have finally heard from Robert Cushman who has met Thomas Weston again.
ROBINSON:	Excellent.
WINSLOW:	Not really. Weston has got nasty.
ELIZABETH:	What do you mean?
WINSLOW:	You know he told us that we could work four days a week for the Merchant Adventurers and two for ourselves?
ELIZABETH:	He's changed it?
WINSLOW:	Now he says that "circumstances have changed" and they can't get a fishing monopoly for our new settlement.
ROBINSON:	But that was all part of the original agreement. There's fish aplenty there. What's the problem?
WINSLOW:	Mr Weston isn't saying, but he does make the point that the London merchants are quite concerned about that and that they are threatening to back out.
BRADFORD:	Meaning?
WINSLOW:	There will be no money unless...
ELIZABETH:	I don't like the sound of this. Unless what?

WINSLOW: Unless we agree to work six days a week instead of four, which means we have no time to till our own fields - if we have any - or work for ourselves in any way.

ROBINSON: And of course, the Lord's Day is sacrosanct. This cannot be broken.

WINSLOW: Indeed. And Weston is perfectly aware of this

ROBINSON: We can't sign that. It's an agreement fitter for thieves and bondslaves than for honest men.

BRADFORD: I agree. Cushman has to go back to Weston and just say No.

WINSLOW: That's the problem. Cushman has already signed.

ELIZABETH: Without coming back to us first?

ROBINSON: That's highly irresponsible

WINSLOW: He wasn't well when we met in London. He couldn't even attend that meeting with Thomas Weston.

BRADFORD: Well we just say No. I personally don't feel bound by what Cushman has agreed. Especially as he did so without reference to us.

WINSLOW: But then the Merchant Adventurers will just pull out and withdraw their money.

BRADFORD: That's a risk we will have to take.

WINSLOW: I don't like it.

ELIZABETH: Neither do I. And we don't know what Weston
                  might do next. I didn't like him much when we
                  met anyway.

BRADFORD: Well I think it's unreasonable to expect us to
                  labour every single day for them. We will never
                  get anything established. We won't even have
                  the time to build houses. Nothing. The hours
                  of work will be worse than here.

WINSLOW: I'm afraid there is more bad news.

BRADFORD: What now?

WINSLOW: Weston hasn't got round to getting the ship yet.

BRADFORD: That at least is a lesser problem. We had already
                  decided we had enough money and expertise to
                  try to get one ourselves through our contacts
                  here.

ROBINSON: Well, you had decided! I am not sure it was put
                  to the vote...

WINSLOW: I think William is right. That is something we
                  can do. At least we can find a ship that will get
                  us to Southampton and if Weston comes up
                  with another, so much the better.

ROBINSON: Was there anything else in Cushman's missive
                  Edward?

WINSLOW: Weston and the other Merchant Adventurers
                  are insisting on adding some other people to
                  our little group. So, there will be a group of
                  non-Separatists there.

BRADFORD: Why?

ELIZABETH: I suppose they are attracted by the profit they might make from all this fish and all those furs.

WINSLOW: Cushman says that some of them do have connections with our people here in Leiden, but a lot of them don't.

BRADFORD: This was never part of the original deal with Weston. What's he doing?

ELIZABETH: The more people he can squash onto a ship, the better for his profits. I just hope we don't end up like those people from Emden.

ROBINSON: Amen to that.

WINSLOW: There's a little news on provisions. Weston has appointed a man called Christopher Martin to supply provisions for the voyage.

ROBINSON: That's something.

WINSLOW: Yes and No. The trouble is that Martin is refusing to co-operate with our people who are also buying provisions for us ...

ELIZABETH: With our money.

WINSLOW: Exactly. Martin is in Southampton. Our people are in London and they have no idea how much Martin is buying in the way of things like salted beef and pork, hardtack, beer, or dried peas. He's just refusing to tell them. And we don't know if he is getting armour or muskets or fishing supplies or even goods that the Indians might like. Things we could exchange for local knowledge or favours.

BRADFORD: It's a mess. But we're just going to have to get
                 on with it.

WINSLOW: I suppose you're right. But it's not ideal.

BRADFORD: Things never are. But we can do something
                 about the ship. So, if you will excuse me, I will
                 begin the search. A couple of useful contacts
                 live near me.

ROBINSON: William Bradford, before you go, I have
                 something I need to tell you. All of you.

WINSLOW: Oh?

ELIZABETH: Pastor Robinson, you are coming with us,
                 aren't you?

ROBINSON: That's just the matter, Mistress Winslow. I
                 have looked deep into my heart. I have prayed,
                 I have asked God for counsel. And in the end,
                 I feel I cannot accompany you.

ELIZABETH: No!

BRADFORD: But why?

ROBINSON: I am needed here. There will still be many
                 hundreds of English Separatists living here
                 in Leiden. I cannot abandon them. I have to
                 attend to their spiritual needs.

ELIZABETH: But what about our spiritual needs?

ROBINSON: You will have Elder Brewster with you. He is
                 more than competent.

ELIZABETH: If he ever turns up!

ROBINSON: William Brewster will meet you in Southampton. Of that, I am sure.

ELIZABETH: Everything seems like shifting sands at the moment. Nothing is certain, our ship, our so-called agreement with Mr Weston, our supplies and now our beloved Pastor.

BRADFORD: Indeed. We all have need of your counsel Pastor Robinson.

WINSLOW: But we have to make the best of it. Elder Brewster is deeply spiritual and we all love him. We cannot take Pastor Robinson from the congregation still remaining here in Leiden. They need him desperately.

BRADFORD: That is true. *[Pause.]* Well I will go and find a ship!

WINSLOW: I'll come with you.

[Exeunt BRADFORD and WINSLOW.]

ROBINSON: Be of good cheer Mistress Winslow.

ELIZABETH: I will try!

ROBINSON: I must away. And try not to worry.

[ROBINSON exits.]

ELIZABETH: Our mad endeavours have just been rendered practically impossible. What are they all thinking of? *[She prays.]* Forgive me for my lack of faith O Lord. And if it be thy will that I should try to dissuade them from this reckless escapade, give me the strength and the powers

of persuasion to bring them all to their senses,
I beseech thee. Amen.

[ELIZABETH exits.]

ACT 1: Scene 7

[The quay at Delftshaven, Holland. Late July 1620. Enter DOROTHY and William BRADFORD. He is trying to drag her towards the ship.]

DOROTHY: *[Distraught and looking behind her.]* My little son. My little darling. I can't leave him, William. I can't.

BRADFORD: But we have said Goodbye to him. We agreed.

DOROTHY: We did not agree. You simply imposed your views on me. As usual. In the name of being "sensible". I can't bear it. I will fetch him. He will come with us

[DOROTHY forces herself free of BRADFORD's arms and begins to run back. BRADFORD chases after her and grabs her.]

BRADFORD: Dorothy you can't do this to him. You can't upset him like this. We've said our goodbyes. Your parents have taken him to their house now. Your mother will be settling him.

DOROTHY: He's nearly three years old. He's healthy. Susanna and William White are bringing Resolved - their little boy.

BRADFORD: Resolved White is five. That's a huge difference.

DOROTHY: And don't forget she is pregnant with the next one.

BRADFORD: That is their business. *[Pause.]* Dorothy, are you...?

DOROTHY: No, I'm not. I would have told you. Anyway,

you should still agree to John coming. He will bear the rigours of a sea voyage much better than being separated from me. *[Pause.]* From us.

BRADFORD: Dorothy please don't do this. The ship will be sailing any minute.

DOROTHY: And is that more important than the welfare of my little boy? You have been so tied up in all the arrangements that you haven't had time to see how much he has grown and how much more aware he is.

BRADFORD: I'm his father Dorothy. Of course, I can see. Just don't accuse me of not caring.

DOROTHY: Well that's how it appears to me. You have put the welfare of the whole congregation over the welfare of your own baby. How could you? How could you?

BRADFORD: Well someone had to organise the ship and the provisions and the crew and keep in touch with what is happening in England at the same time. You have absolutely no idea of what needed to be done Dorothy.

DOROTHY: And you have absolutely no idea of the needs of your own son.

BRADFORD: Please, just get onto the ship Dorothy. We need to leave.

DOROTHY: I tell you William, that I know I will never ever see John's little face again.

BRADFORD: Now you are being ridiculous.

DOROTHY: How dare you? I have this awful feeling that one of us will die before we meet again. *[Screams.]* My son, my son! How can I bear to lose you?

[Enter ELIZABETH and Edward WINSLOW. ELIZABETH runs to DOROTHY.]

ELIZABETH: Dorothy, Dorothy, please don't be so distraught. He will come out when he is a little older. Dorothy!

DOROTHY: *[Sobs.]* I will be dead first. I will never see my little John again. Never, never.

ELIZABETH: Please Dorothy. Come with me. *[She puts her arms around Dorothy.]* I understand what you are going through. Be comforted. You will see him again. Come with me. You need water and rest.

[Exeunt DOROTHY and ELIZABETH.]

BRADFORD: My poor little wife. She can't bear it, the separation from John. She can't accept that it's best for him.

WINSLOW: Did you really have to leave him behind?

BRADFORD: We agreed in Congregation that it should be the strongest and fittest of us who should go to the New World. John is not yet three. And he is delicate. It's hard for me too Winslow.

WINSLOW: I know. *[Pause.]* Perhaps she will be better once we sail. It's a short trip to Southampton.

BRADFORD: I hope so. I love her dearly and I can't bear to see her like this.

WINSLOW: Of course. *[Pause.]* At least we are all loaded up now. I really didn't think we would be able to get Elder Brewster's huge chest on board!

BRADFORD: Or his books!

WINSLOW: And then the Whites insisted on bringing all that butter and cheese.

BRADFORD: I trust Brewster's books were safe from that!

WINSLOW: Don't worry. I oversaw the loading of it. Lovely fresh stuff. *[Pause.]* Is there any more news about what happens when we get to Southampton?

BRADFORD: *[Laughs ruefully.]* Not much. We will meet the others who wish to go with us.

WINSLOW: Strangers?

BRADFORD: Exactly. Many of them will not be of our persuasion.

WINSLOW: Well we knew that.

BRADFORD: And hopefully by that time, our friend Thomas Weston will have found a second ship.

WINSLOW: So we sail in convoy?

BRADFORD: I believe so. *[Pause.]* And I am not sure I'm much looking forward to our next meeting with Weston.

WINSLOW: He's a slippery customer. Elizabeth was right.

BRADFORD: She's very perceptive, your wife.

WINSLOW: So I'm told! Anyway, we need to leave within
              the hour. The tide...

BRADFORD: We are waiting for Pastor Robinson. His
              farewell sermon...

WINSLOW: I hope he gets here soon. *[Pause.]* She's a bonny
              ship. The Speedwell. Good name. You did well
              to get her.

BRADFORD: I had good advice. Ah, here is Pastor Robinson.

WINSLOW: At last. I hope he doesn't go on for too long.

BRADFORD: He knows about tides!

*[Enter ROBINSON with others. BRADFORD and WINSLOW stand
Stage Left and Stage Right respectively.]*

ROBINSON: Loving Christian friends, I do heartily and
              in the Lord salute you. As you know, I have
              enormous affection for you all though I am
              constrained for a while to be bodily absent from
              you. I say constrained: God knowing how
              willingly, and much rather than otherwise, I
              would have borne my part with you in this first
              brunt, were I not by strong necessity held back
              for the present.

              First make sure you repent. Of course, we
              must daily renew our repentance with our
              God, specifically for our sins known, and more
              generally for our unknown trespasses. But
              the Lord calls us in a singular manner upon
              occasions of such difficulty and danger as lieth
              upon you on this fateful day, to a both more

narrow search and a more careful reformation of your ways in his sight.

Next, remember our Church-Covenant whereby we promise and covenant with God and one with another, to receive whatsoever light or truth shall be made known to us from his written Word. And take heed of what you receive for truth; examine and compare and weigh it with other Scriptures before totally accepting it.

In England, in Southampton, you will meet others, strangers even, who wish to go on the voyage. They will share your accommodation on The Speedwell. By all means endeavour to close with the godly party of the Kingdom of England, and rather to study union than division. And don't be afraid to take another Pastor or Teacher, for the flock that has two shepherds is not endangered, but secured by it.

Watchfulness must be had, that we neither at all in our selves do give, no nor easily take offence being given by others. As Christ our Lord teacheth, Matthew Chapter 7, verses 1, 2, and 3.

WINSLOW: "Judge not that ye be not judged"?

ROBINSON: Precisely. And indeed, my own experience confirms, few or none have been found which sooner give offence, then such as easily take it; neither have they ever proved sound and profitable members in societies, which have nourished this touchy humour.

[His audience laughs and applauds.]

> Time and tide wait for no man so I call
> fervently upon the Lord, He who has made the
> heavens and the earth, the sea and all rivers
> and waters, and whose providence is over all
> his works, especially over all his dear children
> that he would so guide and guard you in your
> ways, that we and you may have reason to praise
> His name all the days of your and our lives.

[ROBINSON, tears running down his cheeks, now falls kneeling onto the ground.]

ROBINSON: Fare you well in Him in whom you trust, and
in whom I rest. I am, as you see, an unfeigned
well-wisher of your happy success in this
hopeful voyage.

[Enter Elizabeth and Dorothy. They embrace Robinson followed by Winslow and Bradford. The four now exeunt, with others. Robinson remains kneeling.]

ROBINSON: My children, I commend you with my most
fervent prayers to God and I ask for his
blessings upon you.

[We hear the sounds of the ship departing. ROBINSON continues to kneel, a lone figure, with his arms outstretched. Lights fade. INTERVAL.]

ACT 2: Scene 1

[Rotherhithe Late July 1620. Captain JONES enters from Stage Right and Christopher MARTIN from Stage Left.]

MARTIN: Ah, you must be Captain Jones. Allow me to introduce myself. Christopher Martin. I'm in charge of victualling the ships.

JONES: Good to meet you, Mr Martin. We'll be seeing a lot of each other I dare say.

MARTIN: I certainly hope so. I've had my first look of the ship. The Mayflower you call her? A fine-looking vessel. *[Pause.]* Not in the first flush of youth I would venture?

JONES: *[Laughs.]* You're right. She's had a bonny career crossing the Channel many times laden with wines from France, paid for by the finest English woollens!

MARTIN: A good trade then.

JONES: I would say so. So you're in business?

MARTIN: I've been a merchant all my life. I bought a few shares in the Virginia Company and met Mr Weston through that...

JONES: Weston? Thomas Weston?

MARTIN: That's the one. He recruited me to furnish the ships with supplies.

JONES: He's a busy man! He was the one who chartered the Mayflower for the voyage to America.

MARTIN: Interesting. *[Pause.]* Is your experience limited
                 to the Channel then?

JONES: Certainly not. We've done voyages to Norway,
                 Sweden, the Baltic and...

MARTIN: Norway? What did they want to buy?

JONES: Hats, vinegar, hemp, Spanish salt. A huge
                 variety of things. And later on, we went up to
                 Greenland for a bit of whaling.

MARTIN: Impressive. *[Pause.]* So, you're not from these
                 parts then?

JONES: Born in Harwich.

MARTIN: I'm an Essex man myself. But I don't know
                 Harwich. It's a busy port they tell me.

JONES: Indeed. It's a fine town. But business started to
                 fail and the family was growing, so we decided
                 to settle in Rotherhithe.

MARTIN: Good choice.

JONES: But then trade dried up even here.

MARTIN: Ah yes, the situation in Europe's very unstable.
                 I don't like the sound of that conflict in
                 Austria, Bohemia or wherever it is; it'll be the
                 ruin of many businesses and...

*[MARTIN is interrupted by the arrival of John BILLINGTON and
Stephen HOPKINS.]*

BILLINGTON: Morning Jones. Fine boat. But a bit shabby.
                 Seaworthy is it?

JONES: You clearly don't know much about ships Mr Billington. The Mayflower is checked over constantly. She's an old ship but sturdy and experienced.

BILLINGTON: Didn't mean to give offence. Have you met Stephen Hopkins? Captain Jones of the Mayflower and Christopher Martin, manager and victualler.

JONES: How do you do?

MARTIN: Delighted to meet you Mr Hopkins. Your fame travels far. You have experience of the New World, I think?

HOPKINS: Well if you think that a shipwreck in Bermuda is good experience!

MARTIN: I certainly do. You survived it!

HOPKINS: Well yes. But the four years in Jamestown will probably prove more useful.

MARTIN: I am surprised you want to go back after the experiences you've had.

HOPKINS: There's nothing for me here.

BILLINGTON: What do you mean?

HOPKINS: Work, professional opportunities, that sort of thing.

BILLINGTON: So you're not a religious man then? Unlike some of the passengers we'll be with?

HOPKINS: I'm not one of the Puritan types if that's what
                    you mean? What do they call themselves, the
                    Saints? I just liked the idea of going to Virginia.

MARTIN: Well you'll be seeing enough of the Saints as
                    you call them. There's about fifty, maybe more,
                    coming from Leiden. Religious fanatics. You'll
                    meet them in Southampton.

HOPKINS: What sort of fanatics?

MARTIN: Don't get me wrong. I've had my arguments
                    with the Church myself. I don't like this
                    kneeling business. Too popish for me. My wife
                    and I refused to kneel at Communion last
                    Easter, and my boys were criticised for their
                    answers during training for their confirmation.
                    But these Leideners, they go a bit far in my
                    opinion. They think they have a Covenant
                    with God. And they say they go to America as
                    "Pilgrims". Sheer affectation.

BILLINGTON: Well, I've never been much of a worshipper
                    myself. It's hard enough to get my children
                    inside a Church!

MARTIN: And these people from Leiden are so fussy,
                    so difficult to deal with. I'm a merchant,
                    experienced in buying and selling. They ask me,
                    on their behalf, to get supplies for them. No
                    problem. That's my job. I'm good at it. Know
                    good suppliers. But these "Saints" drive me
                    mad. I can't get a straight answer out of them as
                    to what they want. A couple of them were sent
                    over from Leiden, and are buying equipment
                    and foodstuffs in London. They just don't
                    want to liaise, to co-operate. Too damn sainted
                    in my view. I expect we have bought some of
                    the same stuff.

HOPKINS: Well you can't have enough supplies on a voyage like this. When do we sail Captain?

JONES: Within two days. I need to get a few more crew members.

MARTIN: Big crew, is it?

JONES: We need over thirty before the mast and then another twelve seamen, plus four officers on my staff. We're missing about a dozen. In fact, if you will excuse me Sirs, I need to get on. My quartermaster is bringing over some men for me to interview. Good day to you.

[JONES exits.]

MARTIN: Well I have work to do. We need fresh food for the voyage to Southampton. Sixty-five people on board. That's the latest tally anyway! Good Day sirs. I expect we will meet again very soon.

[MARTIN Exits. We hear the raucous cries of young boys having a goodnatured fight; there is the sound of a dog barking.]

BILLINGTON: That's my boys if I'm not mistaken. Terrorising the town again! *[Calls offstage.]* John! Francis! Just stop that. And leave the dog alone. It's not yours!

HOPKINS: You need to get those boys under control. They'll be a menace on the ship.

BILLINGTON: *[Calls offstage.]* Francis, put those apples down. We haven't paid for them! *[On his exit.]* Francis, you're going to get a good thrashing. I mean it.

[SFX dogs barking and boys yelling. Lights.]

ACT 2: Scene 2

[Southampton Docks. 31st July 3pm. Enter Thomas WESTON Stage Right and William BRADFORD and ELIZABETH and Edward WINSLOW Stage Left.]

WINSLOW: Ah Mr Weston!

WESTON: Well, you took your time arriving. The Mayflower got here two days ago. What took you so long?

BRADFORD: There's nothing we can do about the tides Mr Weston. We left on time. The Speedwell is a nippy little vessel. I trust the Mayflower is equally serviceable.

ELIZABETH: We have met Captain Jones. He looks like a good man. Experienced too.

WESTON: I am glad you approve Mistress Winslow. Now, we need to talk business.

WINSLOW: Ah. The contract...

WESTON: Not so fast, Mr Winslow. Not so fast. There is something else I need to talk to you about first. Something quite delicate.

BRADFORD: Intriguing.

WESTON: I'm not sure that's the word I'd use.

BRADFORD: Explain, if you will.

WESTON: In addition to the other families you will be meeting...

ELIZABETH: The strangers?

WESTON: You may call them what you will Mistress
               Winslow. The Merchant Adventurers were
               obliged to recruit these families since the
               numbers coming from Leiden declined
               - significantly - since we first started our
               discussions.

ELIZABETH: Oh we all understand the need for you to look
               after your profit margin Mr Weston.

WINSLOW: Elizabeth, this doesn't help.

WESTON: Business is business Mr. Winslow and I think
               your missus understands this. Now, as to
               the delicate matter in hand. There are four
               children...

ELIZABETH: Children?

WESTON: Very young children. The family name is
               More. They are from Shropshire. They are here
               without their parents.

ELIZABETH: Are the parents dead? How old are the children?

WESTON: One question at a time, if you please Mistress
               Winslow. Now, if memory serves, the oldest,
               Elinor, is seven and then there are two boys
               Jasper and Richard. The youngest, Mary is
               four.

ELIZABETH: But where are the parents? Dead?

WESTON: In brief, they are the children of Mrs Catherine
               More. Her husband Samuel spent most of his
               time in London. Had an excellent position

- secretary to some privy councillor. I forget the name. Anyway, when Mary was born, he noticed, for the first time, that all the children looked like another man, a neighbour, a man in fact who had been Catherine's fiancé before she was forced to marry Samuel More.

ELIZABETH: He took his time. To notice, I mean.

WESTON: My sentiments exactly Mistress Winslow. I have known Samuel More for years. Never one for being observant, I'll have to admit. And as usual, he dumps the problem on me.

BRADFORD: What do you mean?

WESTON: You may well ask. Samuel snatched them from their mother within weeks of her giving birth to the youngest and dumps them with some of his father's tenants. Their mother was desperate. She went to court. She screamed. She wept. No avail. He was determined to revenge himself on her. And then he hears about this expedition to Virginia. So what does he do? He palms the children off on me! On me sir! He decides that they should be as far removed from their mother as possible to escape her pernicious influence, or so he says. His plan is for them to travel as indentured servants with some of you.

WINSLOW: This is a shocking story.

ELIZABETH: Those poor little children.

BRADFORD: We couldn't possibly treat such young children as servants.

WINSLOW: No, no but we could look after them.

ELIZABETH: I feel for the mother. Surely she has some rights. There must be a way for her to see her children again. And they will be needing her desperately.

WESTON: There's no going back Mistress Winslow. The case was settled in court. *[Pause.]* So you are willing to take them?

BRADFORD: We don't have much choice.

WINSLOW: Elizabeth and I can take care of one of them.

ELIZABETH: Of course.

WINSLOW: There will be other families who will be pleased to look after them. What about you and Dorothy?

BRADFORD: No, no. It would hurt her even more. *[To Weston.]* Where are they now?

WESTON: Here, in Southampton. I was obliged to travel with them and accommodate them. You will see them presently.

BRADFORD: Well that's settled then. We will find people to look after them. *[Pause.]* And now we need to talk business.

WESTON: Yes indeed, I have here the contract - the amended contract -

BRADFORD: The one stipulating that we should work all week for the Adventurers?

WESTON: *[Silkily.]* The very same. *[Producing papers.]* Now
                   I believe there was a little misunderstanding
                   in Leiden, but I am sure, Mr Bradford that
                   you will see that this new clause is in fact very
                   reasonable. As devout believers you will, I am
                   confident, shy away from any semblance of
                   breach of promise. So, all we have to do Mr
                   Bradford is to sign here, confirming what we
                   had in essence agreed. And what your agent Mr
                   Cushman signed on your behalf.

BRADFORD: Cushman had no authority to do that.

WESTON: That is none of my business as I am sure you
                   will appreciate. So, if you and Mr Winslow
                   wouldn't mind signing, I really have a lot more
                   business to attend to.

BRADFORD: No.

WESTON: I beg your pardon

BRADFORD: We cannot put our names to a document that
                   will force our people to work in this way. When
                   are we supposed to till our own fields, or even
                   build houses?

WESTON: I am sure you will have ways and means Mr
                   Bradford. Now, time is running out. We have
                   to sail within days. I need your signature.

BRADFORD: Again, the answer is no. The contract is unjust
                   and unfair.

WESTON: But Mr Cushman agreed it.

BRADFORD: Mr Cushman was unwell and he acted without
                   authority. I repeat, the answer is No. Please go
                   back to the Adventurers and ask them to agree

more reasonable terms. We need two days - or at the very least one day - a week to labour for ourselves.

WESTON: And as I have repeatedly explained Mr Bradford, the situation has changed. Markets are uncertain and trade is weak. The Adventurers do not have gigantic pockets. Will you sign?

BRADFORD: For the last time Mr Weston, the answer is no.

WESTON: *[Angry.]* In that case, I shall leave you. You will now have to stand on your own feet. You have just argued yourselves out of a very large sum of money. *[Gathers papers.]* I will send the children to you. Good day.

[WESTON exits.]

ELIZABETH: That went well!

BRADFORD: It's serious. It means he is not going to let us have the last payment.

WINSLOW: Which means we can't pay suppliers for the stores and equipment for the voyage.

ELIZABETH: But you were right to stand up to him William. *[Pause.]* I suppose the only way to get a little money is to sell off some of the butter and cheese we brought from Holland...

WINSLOW: But we will need that ourselves.

ELIZABETH: Not necessarily. Butter and cheese are luxuries really. We brought over a lot - a huge amount - to remind us of Holland. It will sell well. Come on down to the market with me. Let's see.

[Exeunt.]

ACT 2: Scene 3

[Southampton Docks. 5th August 1620. Enter DOROTHY and William BRADFORD with ELIZABETH Winslow.]

BRADFORD: Both the ships sail today. I had hoped the Speedwell might sail a little later after the Mayflower to give Elder Brewster more time to get here.

DOROTHY: I really thought he would be here by now.

ELIZABETH: I still have a feeling he will manage to find us. Probably just as we are about to embark. And he will have no idea that we were so worried. Edward went to see whether he was on the other side of town.

BRADFORD: We really need him. Especially as we are without Pastor Robinson. We have no spiritual leader. Ah, there is one possibility, I could try negotiating again for an extra day so that...

[Enter MARY and William BREWSTER. The characters onstage all embrace each other.]

BREWSTER: My friends, my brothers and sisters, how good it is to see you. I fear we are a little late...

ELIZABETH: Just a little!

BREWSTER: But you never doubted we would come? How we have missed you all.

ELIZABETH: And we have missed you. We brought your desk with us!

DOROTHY: Are all the family with you?

MARY: Just the two youngest sons.

ELIZABETH: Love and Wrestling?

MARY: You have a good memory!

ELIZABETH: Well, those names are somewhat... memorable!

BRADFORD: We were so worried about you. We had no idea where you were.

MARY: We had to flit from safe house to safe house and then we finally reached England - about three months ago. We've been in the North. People have been so good.

BREWSTER: Southampton is an interesting place. We have met some of our new companions on the voyage.

ELIZABETH: The "strangers"?

BREWSTER: Most of them godly and devout people. Some of them perhaps...

[BREWSTER breaks off as John BILLINGTON runs on.]

BILLINGTON: John! Francis! Come back here this minute. We're about to sail! [*Notices the others.*] Excuse me. Have you seen two young boys - one thirteen years old and the younger one eleven? Right tearaways they are, though I have to say it myself of my own sons!

BRADFORD: Sorry no. We have seen no-one. You are ...?

BILLINGTON: John Billington at your service. Sailed from Rotherhithe to Southampton on the Mayflower. I haven't met you before. Are you

the godly ones? Sailed on the Speedwell from
Holland?

BREWSTER: Well we try to do the Lord's work my son.
William Brewster at your service.

BILLINGTON: Ah, you are the gentleman they were waiting
for. Been in hiding have you?

BREWSTER: Well that sort of thing!

BILLINGTON: *[Speaking as Christopher MARTIN enters.]* Well if
it ain't Mr Martin coming to hurry us all along.
We'll be right with you Mr Martin. Just lost my
boys. Again. I'll be right back.

[BILLINGTON exits.]

MARTIN: Here, Billington! Oh what's the use? If he
misses the boat, it's his own fault. Mr Brewster,
I thought I told you and your wife to get on the
Speedwell immediately. We are loading now.
Sailing in two hours.

ELIZABETH: Ah! two hours to sell the rest of the cheese!
Excuse me.

[ELIZABETH exits.]

MARTIN: Where's she off to?

BRADFORD: Don't worry she knows what she's doing.

MARTIN: Well, she'd better or I won't answer for the
consequences. Now then Brewster, what's the
story?

BRADFORD: *[Shocked.]* He should be addressed as Elder
Brewster

MARTIN:	Elder! Younger! What do I care? I have a job of work to do which is to load two ships in the next two hours. Now Brewster, get yourself and your wife onto the Speedwell immediately. Your sons are on board.
BREWSTER:	Thank you for the intelligence.
MARTIN:	And they'd better watch their manners. I asked them their names. They said they were called Love and Wrestling! I ask you. What kind of fool do they think I am? I gave them a cuff about the ears to teach them a lesson, but they didn't change their story.
MARY:	Mr Martin, these are their real names. Names to remind us of the love of God and of the struggle we wage each day against the forces of evil. We have a daughter called Fear who ...
MARTIN:	*[Incredulous.]* Fear? Fear?
MARY:	Indeed sir. She was born during the height of the persecution against Separatist congregations like ours. When we were still in the North of England, years before the escape to Holland.
MARTIN:	Well you could have fooled me Mistress. Didn't mean to cause offence.
BREWSTER:	None taken.
DOROTHY:	Mary, Edward was looking for you in town and feared you would not be in time for the departure.
MARY:	Well, as you can see, we just managed it!

MARTIN: All right. All right. You can gossip all you like
                   on board. Get yourselves on. Now!

BREWSTER: We will see you later.

[BREWSTER exits with Mary.]

MARTIN: And you two, it's not helpful just standing
                   around. You'd better follow your... *[Sneeringly.]*
                   ...Elder.

[MARTIN exits.]

DOROTHY: What a horrible man.

BRADFORD: Cushman warned me about Christopher
                   Martin. He said that Martin treats our people
                   with such scorn and contempt as if they were
                   not fit to wipe his shoes.

DOROTHY: He's not coming with us on the Speedwell is
                   he?

BRADFORD: Fortunately, not. He's the so-called governor of
                   the Mayflower so we don't really have to deal
                   with him until we get to Virginia.

DOROTHY: What a relief.

[Exeunt.]

ACT 2: Scene 4

[Bayards Cove, Dartmouth. August 12th 1620. Enter MARY, BREWSTER, DOROTHY, BRADFORD, ELIZABETH, and WINSLOW.]

WINSLOW: That was a lucky escape. I really thought we wouldn't make Dartmouth.

DOROTHY: She was leaking like a sieve.

BRADFORD: I don't understand it. We were assured again and again back in Leiden that the Speedwell was one of the most reliable ships they had seen in years. I should have asked more questions, probed deeper ...

BREWSTER: Don't blame yourself my son

BRADFORD: But the water was pouring in through the planks. I've never seen anything like it.

ELIZABETH: It reminded me of a leaking dyke back in Holland!

BREWSTER: But we are safe. And this is a very pleasant area of Dartmouth.

MARY: Indeed. It's known as Bayards Cove.

WINSLOW: The mayor says we can camp here while the repairs are done.

DOROTHY: How long will they take?

BRADFORD: The carpenters said at least ten days.

MARY: Ten days? As much as that?

BRADFORD: That includes allowing for the wind to change.
                    One never really knows.

MARY: But we will get through all our provisions
                    before we have even left England.

WINSLOW: Well at least we have been allowed off the ship.

ELIZABETH: What do you mean?

WINSLOW: Martin the Martinet is refusing to let anyone
                    off the *Mayflower*. They have to stay on board.
                    There isn't even anything wrong with the
                    Mayflower.

ELIZABETH: So why do they have to stay on board?

WINSLOW: Because Martin says so.

BRADFORD: *[Savagely.]* He enjoys the power.

BREWSTER: My son, my son, let us not be judges one of
                    another. Let us give thanks for our deliverance.
                    Come together and let us pray.

[All form a circle.]

BREWSTER: We thank thee O God for our salvation and
                    for our safety here in this beautiful place. We
                    pray that we may be watchful and kind. Teach
                    us that to look after one another is a sure and
                    certain way of praising thee. We ask that we use
                    our time in Dartmouth in a prayerful way. In
                    the name of God.

ALL: Amen.

BRADFORD: Thank you Elder Brewster. I was grievously in
                    need of that.

BREWSTER: I know. You are under a lot of pressure brother. Now who's coming to find a good place to camp for a few days. Beautiful weather. Very attractive place. God has certainly blessed us.

[Exeunt BREWSTER and MARY.]

WINSLOW: *[To ELIZABETH.]* Are you coming?

ELIZABETH: I'll stay with Dorothy.

BRADFORD: We won't be long. Dorothy?

[BRADFORD tries to kiss DOROTHY but she turns away. Exeunt BRADFORD and WINSLOW.]

ELIZABETH: It's not his fault, the ship leaking.

DOROTHY: I know. I know. I feel dreadful but I can't forgive him.

ELIZABETH: This is still about baby John?

DOROTHY: I think of him day and night. William never ever really listened to me.

ELIZABETH: I know. He seemed to change while he was organising everything in Leiden. All the pressure was on him. Edward tried to help, but really the responsibility was William's. And he's exhausted. You can see.

DOROTHY: Yes I know.

ELIZABETH: I mean I have never heard him speak ill of anyone but he was pretty sharp about Christopher Martin. That just shows he's almost at the end of his tether.

DOROTHY: I know I'm being selfish. I'll try to forgive him.

ELIZABETH: It's so hard, I never really wanted to come either. So much is unknown. Very few people have any experience of America - apart from Stephen Hopkins, one of the strangers. He'll be useful. *[Pause.]* I did try to talk Edward out of it you know.

DOROTHY: I had no idea.

ELIZABETH: It didn't work. He's desperate to go, so I have almost succeeded in reconciling myself.

DOROTHY: I wish they had agreed to let John Smith come with us. William bought his map of New England. It is superb. He has more experience than anyone we know. He was really keen to go back when they met him. And he especially wanted to go to Massachusetts. He described it as "the paradise of those parts."

ELIZABETH: I think I know why they turned Mr Smith down.

DOROTHY: Really?

ELIZABETH: He knows too much. And he would have tried to advise them. And as you know very well Dorothy, godly men don't like being told what to do!

DOROTHY: *[Laughs and laughs.]* That's wonderful Elizabeth. And so true. *[Pause.]* You know, I can't remember when I laughed like that. It's done me good.

ELIZABETH: So you'll try and forgive William?

DOROTHY: Yes, I'll try.

ELIZABETH: And this is a pretty place and we have the most glorious weather. The calm before the storm. Come Dorothy.

[Exeunt.]

ACT 2: Scene 5

[Plymouth Docks. 16th September 1620. Enter DOROTHY and ELIZABETH.]

ELIZABETH: Mary Brewster! Mary Brewster!

[Enter MARY.]

ELIZABETH: How are the negotiations going? Dorothy and I
                    were not allowed to be present.

MARY: *[Laughs.]* I was there but certainly not expected
                    to speak!

ELIZABETH: So what's been decided?

MARY: I think we are going to have to abandon the
                    Speedwell.

DOROTHY: But it's a lovely ship. Can't they repair it again?

MARY: The shipwright says there is too much damage
                    to her, and it is too risky. She has let us down
                    twice.

ELIZABETH: And we were doing so well. Two hundred miles
                    beyond Land's End. We were really on our way.

MARY: I can't bear the amount of time just wasted.
                    It is already mid-September. The weather will
                    start to get stormy. *[Pause.]* I am not sure I am
                    supposed to tell you this but ...

ELIZABETH: Yes?

MARY: There is a suggestion of foul play.

DOROTHY: No!

MARY: The Speedwell was a good ship and in fine
                repair when it was bought in Leiden - better
                really than the Mayflower. So two leaks within
                such a short space of time is very odd.

DOROTHY: What are they suggesting?

MARY: The shipwright believes that the ship was
                overmasted. So there was too much strain on
                the rest of the ship and the seams between the
                planks just opened out. Well, you saw what
                happened. The water just poured through.

DOROTHY: Why would anyone do that? It's almost as if
                someone was trying to stop us getting there.

MARY: No-one knows. There are so many different
                groups wishing to establish themselves in
                America. So many conflicting interests. Huge
                amounts of money at stake.

ELIZABETH: And perhaps the shipwright was just mistaken.

MARY: Well, this is Plymouth. They do know about
                ships here!

ELIZABETH: True. So what happens now? We can't get
                another ship.

MARY: They are talking about getting everyone onto
                the Mayflower.

DOROTHY: There won't be enough room.

MARY: Some Pilgrims have already volunteered to
                stand down.

DOROTHY: But people have given up everything to be here.
                Sold houses, given up employment, borrowed
                money - everything to start a new life.

MARY: It seems that some have had a change of heart.

ELIZABETH: This also means we have the "pleasure" of that
                nice gentleman Christopher Martin giving us
                orders the whole time. The so-called governor
                of the Mayflower.

MARTIN: [*From offstage.*] Anybody not on the Mayflower
                within the hour gets left behind.

ELIZABETH: Talk of the devil.

[Enter MARTIN.]

MARTIN: Didn't you hear the order?

MARY: No.

MARTIN: You were told to be attentive.

MARY: We'll be right there.

MARTIN: You'd better. The wind has changed and
                Captain Jones says we must take advantage. Off
                you go. At the double.

[Exit.]

ELIZABETH: Such a nice polite man!

MARY: I never thought we would be leaving from
                Plymouth. This time, it feels serious. We are
                departing England - for good.

DOROTHY: And may the Lord God have mercy on us.

[Exeunt.]

MARTIN: *[From offstage, screaming.]* All aboard! All aboard!

[SFX sounds of the ship departing.]

ACT 2: Scene 6

[On the deck of the Mayflower. October 1620. ELIZABETH and Edward WINSLOW, MARY and William BREWSTER, DOROTHY, and William BRADFORD are seated in a circle. They are singing part of Psalm 107 verses 23-30.]

{23}   They that go down to the sea in ships: and occupy their business in great waters;

{24}   These men see the works of the Lord: and his wonders in the deep.

{25}   For at his word the stormy wind ariseth: which lifteth up the waves thereof.

{26}   They are carried up to the heaven, and down again to the deep: their soul melteth away because of the trouble.

{27}   They reel to and fro, and stagger like a drunken man: and are at their wits' end.

{28}   So when they cry unto the Lord in their trouble: he delivereth them out of their distress.

{29}   For he maketh the storm to cease: so that the waves thereof are still.

{30}   Then are they glad, because they are at rest: and so he bringeth them unto the haven where they would be.

[Enter Thomas HENLEY.]

HENLEY: Ain't you got your sea legs yet then? All this talk about staggering around like drunken men? You landlubbers you. I expect I'll have to throw all your dead bodies overboard by the end of the voyage. *[Laughs raucously.]*

BREWSTER: Could you give us some peace? We are trying to carry out our daily worship.

SAILOR: Looks like you'll need it old man. Not much experience of the sea then?

BREWSTER: More than you think.

HENLEY: And look at her! *[Points at Dorothy.]* White as a sheet. Not nice, is it? The seasickness?

DOROTHY: *[Stoutly.]* I'm naturally pale. Please attend to your duties.

HENLEY: Hark at her, laying down the law. And don't say you haven't had the seasickness yet. I've seen you and the other young lady. You won't find me there. Healthy as anything me. Thomas Henley at your service!

BREWSTER: I congratulate you on your fitness sir. Now perhaps you can let us have some peace.

HENLEY: As you wish squire. But don't say I didn't warn you.

[HENLEY exits laughing.]

BREWSTER: Shall we start again?

{28} So when they cry unto the Lord in their trouble: he delivereth them out of their distress.

{29} For he maketh the storm to cease: so that the waves thereof are still.

{30} Then are they glad, because they are at rest: and so he bringeth them unto the haven where they would be.

[The singing is interrupted by shouts.]

CREW: *[Offstage.]* Man overboard! Man overboard!

BRADFORD: Who is it? Who is it? We should go and help!

[BRADFORD rushes off with WINSLOW.]

BREWSTER: Let us pray for that man, whoever he is. God, the father of all, spare we pray thee the life of this person. Help those who are trying to save him. Lord have mercy on his soul.

ALL: Amen.

CREW: *[Offstage.]* Heave Ho! Heave Ho!

                    Hang onto the rope John Howland!

                    Nearly there!

                    Yes, we've got him!

                    Mind your backs!

                    Lay him down, gently now, on the deck there!

[BRADFORD and WINSLOW run back.]

WINSLOW: It was John Howland, one of the young servants. Strong as an ox. He got sucked right down, but then managed to grab one of the ropes attached to the topsail dragging along in the water; and then he was pulled about ten feet under the water, but he just clung onto that rope, and they managed to winch him up.

BRADFORD: Miraculous to see. He never let go. Determined to live, that one.

ELIZABETH: That's wonderful. He was very lucky.

MARY: Yes. He could so easily have drowned.

BREWSTER: And so we give thanks unto the Lord.

ALL: Amen.

[The women drift upstage.]

DOROTHY: It's lovely being up here on deck.

MARY: It's so fresh and breezy. And we're away from
                 those horrible smells between decks. And all
                 that rubbish. And people's possessions lying
                 everywhere.

ELIZABETH: I don't want to go below, but I think I should.
                 I'm worried about little Elinor More.

MARY: What's wrong with her?

ELIZABETH: All the More children want their mother of
                 course but she doesn't want to do anything.
                 When I suggested she come on deck with me,
                 she didn't want to. Prefers to stay in that fetid
                 atmosphere between decks. She just sits there.

MARY: That's strange. I left the two younger children
                 playing happily.

ELIZABETH: The little ones don't remember their mother
                 Catherine but Elinor does. She was just old
                 enough. She remembers her mother screaming
                 and crying and demanding to see her and her
                 brothers and sister. And not being allowed to.
                 Just so cruel. It's heartbreaking.

MARY: Poor little girl. That's terrible. I'll come with
                 you.

[Exeunt ELIZABETH and MARY.]

BREWSTER: I don't like the look of that weather. It's
                 beginning to rain.

WINSLOW: And get rough. Ouch! That was a huge lurch.
                 Let's get below before we fall overboard!

[Exeunt WINSLOW and BREWSTER.]

BRADFORD: *[Puts his arms round Dorothy who hugs him back.]*
                 Can you forgive me yet?

DOROTHY: I think I could, maybe.

BRADFORD: Really?

DOROTHY: I know you did it for baby John. I miss him
                 terribly and I worry about him but ...

BRADFORD: We have each other. I love you Dorothy.

DOROTHY: And I love you. It's nice standing here in the
                 rain, on deck, with no-one else around, in your
                 arms. Strangely peaceful.

BRADFORD: *[Kisses her.]* You look like a wet little kitten.
                 Shall we get back down?

DOROTHY: Not just yet. In a minute. William?

BRADFORD: What is it my love?

DOROTHY: Today, I'm feeling a little brighter. I don't know
                 why. I like rain - and I love the sea. But William,
                 sometimes, things feel very black. Sometimes
                 I feel so far away from baby John and I fear I

will never see him. And then I can't seem to do anything at all. I don't like those sad, sad days. But they still happen.

BRADFORD: I know. But I'm here. I'll look after you. You know that.

[DOROTHY rests her head on BRADFORD's chest.]

DOROTHY: I never doubted it. Not really. But now the rain really is coming down. Shall we ...?

BRADFORD: Come on then.

[Exeunt hand in hand.]

ACT 2: Scene 7

[The Mayflower: On Deck. Early November 1620. SFX strong winds and heavy seas. There is a storm raging. ELIZABETH and DOROTHY are on deck. Captain JONES runs on with MARTIN.]

JONES: Are all the sails furled?

CREW: *[Offstage.]* Aye Aye Captain.

JONES: Everything must be cleared from the deck. The gales are going to get worse. I'm setting the ship to leeward. Too rough to do anything else.

MARTIN: What are you two doing up here? Didn't you hear the Captain? Get back down if you want to know what's good for you.

ELIZABETH: We were up for air and...

DOROTHY: And we are upset...

MARTIN: No time to get upset.

DOROTHY: William Button has just died. He was only twenty one.

JONES: Sorry to hear that Mistress Bradford. I've lost a good crew member too. A difficult man, no manners, but good on the rigging.

ELIZABETH: I think I know who you mean - Thomas Henley?

MARTIN: How do you know that young lady?

[JONES, not listening to this, walks around the deck, checking that nothing is in the way. He calls to the crew.]

JONES: That sail is not tied down properly. It needs to be re-done. Won't work like that.

CREW: *[Offstage.]* Aye Aye Captain!

ELIZABETH: He was up here tormenting us many times when we were trying to hold our daily services. And now it seems that the just hand of God is upon him.

MARTIN: You people have a very strange idea of the Almighty.

JONES: The winds are strengthening. Martin, please make sure that all the passengers are below. They must stay below until further orders. Nothing and nobody is to come on deck.

[JONES exits.]

MARTIN: You heard what the Captain said. Be off with you and make sure everyone obeys the order.

ELIZABETH: *[Mockingly.]* Aye Aye Sir.

[Exeunt.]

ACT 2: Scene 8

[November 20th 1620, morning. A calm and beautiful morning. JONES, MARTIN and HOPKINS are on the poop deck.]

CREW: *[Offstage.]* Land ahoy! Land ahoy!

[SFX birdsong.]

JONES: It's Cape Cod.

MARTIN: Cape Cod? Captain, we can't stay here. We have no patent. The lands agreed are way South. In the mouth of the Hudson River.

HOPKINS: We need to make for the Hudson Captain. Otherwise, there will be huge difficulties with the Merchant Adventurers.

JONES: Looks like the wind is heading us South anyway.

MARTIN :   How far is the Hudson?

JONES: Two hundred miles. Perhaps more. But the wind is with us.

HOPKINS: How long will that take us Captain?

JONES: If the wind holds, a couple of days. Maybe more.

HOPKINS: Do you know this coast, Captain? Are there charts?

JONES: Not for this stretch. A couple of the crew have been before. Stout fellows. *[Exit.]*

HOPKINS: *[Disbelievingly.]* He's sailing blind...

MARTIN: *[With irony.]* Join the prayer meeting Hopkins! I'm sure you will be very welcome...

HOPKINS: *[In the same tone.]* That's very kind of you Mr Martin, but I'm not sure it is for the likes of me!

[Exeunt. BLACKOUT.]

ACT 2: Scene 9

[The Mayflower: On Deck November 20th 1620, 3pm. Enter JONES and stands on the poop deck, towards the back of the ship, looking anxiously starboard / stage left.]

JONES: Depth?

CREW: *[Offstage.]* Still a hundred- and twenty-feet Captain.

JONES: Good. Keep it that way.

[SFX ship lurching.]

What was that? The tide's changed!

CREW: *[Offstage. Shouts.]* Aye sir. The tide is running against us now Captain.

JONES: *[Also shouting.]* We've lost the wind too. Completely dropped. Leadsman, keep calling the depth. The depth, man! Quick, give me the depth.

CREW: *[Offstage.]* We've gone to three hundred feet already.

JONES: Unbelievable. Impossible in that time. Measure again.

CREW: Yes Captain;

[Enter MARTIN.]

MARTIN: What's going on?

JONES: Can't talk now. *[To crew.]* Well? What is it?

CREW: It's the same Captain. Three hundred feet.

JONES: We're way off where we should be. Continue to measure.

CREW: Aye Captain.

[SFX the ship lurching, creaking planks.]

MARTIN: I don't like that sound.

JONES: And the wind's gone. We have no wind.

MARTIN: What's that roar? It can't be ...

CREW: The breakers! The breakers! Never seen anything like this Captain.

JONES: Ah! We're at Pollock Rip. We must be. Why didn't I see that before?

MARTIN: *[Shouting.]* Pollock what? Can't hear a word you're saying.

JONES: *[Shouting.]* Pollock Rip. No time for conversation Christopher Martin. We're caught in churning waters - a giant whirlpool. It'll take the devil to get us out. Warn the passengers to stay below. I'm going to try to anchor her.

[Martin exits.]

MARTIN: *[Offstage. Shouting.]* Bradford! William Bradford! Come up to the poop deck! Now!

[BRADFORD enters.]

BRADFORD: What's going on? God save us! What's happening?

ELIZABETH: *[Offstage. Shouts.]* Help, help, what's happening?

DOROTHY: *[Offstage. Also shouting.]* We're going to drown! We're going to drown!

MARY: *[Offstage. Also shouting.]* God save us! God Save us!

[SFX the deafening sounds of breakers.]

BRADFORD: *[Shouts.]* Where are we?

JONES: Pollock Rip.

BRADFORD: What?

JONES: Pollock Rip. Notorious. We're thoroughly entangled among dangerous shoals.

BRADFORD: Shoals? Fish?

JONES: No, man! Sand bars. Ridges. Forcing the waves higher. Can't you hear the sound of the breakers?

BRADFORD: Of course, I can! Never heard anything like this Captain. Roaring without end.

JONES: All I can do is to try to hold her and then extricate her. Please endeavour to keep the passengers calm.

BRADFORD: Aye Aye Captain.

[BRADFORD exits. BLACKOUT.]

ACT 2: Scene 10

[The Mayflower. On Deck November 20th 1620, Two hours later. 5pm.]

CREW: *[Offstage.]* The wind is changing again Captain.

JONES: That's better. A good wind coming from the South. Nothing for it. We're going back North. Back to Cape Cod. Call Bradford.

CREW: *[Offstage.]* Mr. Bradford! Mr. Bradford!

[BRADFORD enters.]

JONES: Mr Bradford, your belief in God has been vindicated. The wind has turned.

BRADFORD: We are out of the shoals?

JONES: Just out. By the mercy of God. We're going back North. Back to Cape Cod.

BRADFORD: But we have no right, no patent to any of the land in the North.

JONES: It's either that or death by drowning. No argument. You'll have to talk to the Adventurers.

BRADFORD: Right.

JONES: There is one hour of daylight left. I will go north as long as I have the light. Then I'm planning to heave to, a few miles off the coast. We'll wait for dawn before landing.

BRADFORD: Good work Captain. I'll tell them

[BRADFORD exits.]

ACT 2: Scene 11

*[The Mayflower's Great Cabin. November 21st 1620, Morning. MARY
and William BREWSTER, DOROTHY and William BRADFORD are
all present along with John BILLINGTON and Stephen HOPKINS.]*

HOPKINS: That's totally unacceptable. We can't go North.
                   We have no patent for any lands in Cape Cod.
                   I signed up to go to Virginia. And that's where
                   I intend to go.

BRADFORD: Captain Jones is in charge. And don't forget he
                   rescued us from Pollock Rip.

BILLINGTON: He had no business putting us there!

BRADFORD: I would like to see you do a better job Mr
                   Billington.

BILLINGTON: No need to get nasty Mr Bradford. Didn't
                   expect that sort of sentiment from a religious
                   man like yourself.

HOPKINS: Bradford, you do realise that those of us who
                   are not from Leiden are not bound by the same
                   rules as you ? Since we are not now going to
                   Virginia as we all expected, we have no patent
                   and we are not bound by anything. Essentially
                   we can do as we like when we land. You have
                   no right to command us.

BILLINGTON: Couldn't put that better myself Mr Hopkins.
                   He's right Bradford. Those of us who joined
                   at Southampton have nothing to do with you
                   Separatists, whatever you call yourselves.

BREWSTER: Sirs, sirs. Let us look at this reasonably. We are
                   about to land in a new country. We need some
                   sort of understanding amongst ourselves as to

how we are going to organise our settlement. In my view whether you are from Leiden or Essex, makes no difference. We are all here, in the same ship and it is in all our interests to agree on a modus vivendi.

BILLINGTON: What's that in English Elder Brewster?

BREWSTER: Pardon Mr Billington. I mean a set of rules and ways of working that we can all agree on. Nothing in too much detail. Just a framework that will help us establish a settlement.

HOPKINS: Do you have anything in mind Elder Brewster?

BREWSTER: I have had a few thoughts and ideas. And Pastor Robinson ...

HOPKINS: Who's he?

BREWSTER: The minister of our congregation in Leiden. He thought deeply on what we might need to do. And I drafted a short document, inspired by his ideas, that I would humbly ask you all to consider.

BILLINGTON: *[Mollified.]* Well that seems reasonable. What do you think Mr Hopkins?

HOPKINS: Let's hear it.

BREWSTER: I have the draft here. *[Reads.]* "Having undertaken for the glory of God and the advancement of the Christian faith and honour of our King and country, a voyage to plant the first colony in the northern parts of Virginia, do these present solemnly and mutually in the presence of God and one of

another, covenant and combine ourselves
together into a civil body politic, for our better
ordering and preservation, and furtherance
of the ends aforesaid; and by virtue hereof
to enact, constitute and frame such just and
equal laws, ordinances, acts, constitutions and
offices, from time to time, as shall be thought
most meet and convenient for the general good
of the colony, unto which we promise all due
submission and obedience."

HOPKINS: I like it. Not too much detail. Just enough.

[SFX a tremendous sound.]

BRADFORD: What's that? I'll go and see.

[BRADFORD exits.]

HOPKINS: So what do we do now Elder Brewster?

BREWSTER: I propose that every man signs this compact.
                    William Bradford will call the names and we
                    will all wait our turns to sign.

BILLINGTON: I agree.

ALL: So be it.

[BRADFORD enters.]

BRADFORD: Captain Jones has anchored us. We have
                    arrived in the New World. In Provincetown!

ALL: *[Cheering.]* God be praised! Thank the Lord!

BREWSTER: Praise be to God who has both brought us
                    here. May we be worthy of his great goodness
                    to us and at all times endeavour to do His will.

ALL: Amen

BREWSTER: And now, we sign.

BRADFORD: William Brewster, you must sign first.

[All five male actors line up. They will stand in for the forty one men who actually signed. So each actor will sign the document about eight times. ELIZABETH, DOROTHY, and MARY watch in silence.]

BRADFORD: William Brewster, and then ...

BREWSTER: Bradford, sign now. I will call your name. William Bradford.

[Bradford signs.]

                   Good.

BRADFORD: Stephen Hopkins, John Billington, Isaac Allerton, John Alden, Myles Standish, John Carver, Samuel Fuller, Christopher Martin, William Mullins, William White, Richard Warren, John Howland, Edward Tilley, John Tilley, Francis Cooke, Thomas Rogers, Thomas Tinker, John Rigsdale, Edward Fuller, John Turner, Francis Eaton, James Chilton, John Crackstone, Moses Fletcher, John Goodman, Degory Priest' Thomas Williams, Edward Winslow, Gilbert Winslow, Edmund Margesson, Peter Browne, Richard Britteridge, George Soule, Richard Clarke, Richard Gardiner, John Allerton, Thomas English, Edward Doty, Edward Leister.

BREWSTER: Thank you. And now, let us go out to see the country to which God has brought us.

ALL: Amen.

[Exeunt.]

EPILOGUE

[The Company reassembles as in the last scene.]

DOROTHY :   The fitter and stronger men of the Mayflower went ashore in small boats to find somewhere safer and more appealing than sandy Provincetown. The women for the most part stayed on the ship. Within four weeks, the search party had found the site of what to was to become Plymouth Massachusetts.

ELIZABETH: William Bradford returned from this trip to the appalling news that his wife Dorothy was dead. Her body had been found floating by the side of the ship as it lay in Provincetown Bay.

[DOROTHY now turns and walks upstage, her back to the audience. BRADFORD comes forward downstage.]

MARY: Bradford never really talked about it, but years later he wrote:

BRADFORD: Faint not, poor soul, in God still trust,
                Fear not the things thou suffer must;
                For whom he loves he doth chastise,
                And then all tears wipes from their eyes.

[BRADFORD bows his head and turns back to his place.]

MARY: Edward Winslow's spirited wife Elizabeth also died in March 1621. Her intelligence and robust assertiveness belied a somewhat delicate physical constitution.

[ELIZABETH now walks upstage, her back to the audience.]

MARY: Many people died between landing and the
                         beginning of the next year's spring, including
                         Elinor More, and her young siblings Jasper
                         and Mary. However, the six-year-old Richard
                         More not only survived, but lived well into his
                         seventies, leaving many descendants.

WINSLOW: The town of Plymouth expanded and a treaty
                         was signed between the new settlers and
                         Massasoit, the King of the Pokanoket tribe
                         part of the Wampanoag tribal federation. This
                         ensured a peace lasting thirty years.

BREWSTER: John Howland, the young servant who had
                         been rescued from the sea lived well, and had
                         ten children with his wife Elizabeth, and no
                         fewer than eighty-eight grandchildren!

MARY: William Bradford served as Governor for thirty
                         years.

BREWSTER: Edward Winslow named his first house
                         Careswell in memory of his parents' house in
                         Droitwich Worcestershire.

MARY: And people continued to arrive. Merchant
                         Adventurer Richard Andrewes who was a
                         major investor in the Mayflower decided to
                         leave behind his life and career in the City of
                         London. Unlike the dastardly Thomas Weston,
                         he was sympathetic to the religious views of the
                         Pilgrims. He left England in 1622 and settled
                         in Massachusetts

BREWSTER: Years later Bradford wrote:

BRADFORD: They had... no friends to welcome them nor
                         inns to entertain or refresh their weather-

beaten bodies; no houses or much less towns to repair to, to seek for succour... What could now sustain them, but the spirit of God and His Grace? May not and ought not the children of these fathers rightly say: Our fathers were Englishmen which came over this great ocean, and were ready to perish in this wilderness, but they cried unto the Lord, and He heard their voice and looked on their adversity.

[FINIS.]

An Introduction To A Couple Of Adapted Monologues From The Script, Suggested For Use As Audition Pieces

These shortish speeches could be used by actors as audition speeches. When we audition actors, we normally give them a couple of pages of the text to prepare. They do not have to be off-book - merely familiar with the text. Both the director, Kenneth Michaels, and I have been on the other side in auditions. We have both suffered the rather harsh, rushed atmosphere of some (not all) professional auditions, and we try very hard to give all actors a more pleasant experience. We find that both agents and actors respond well. We also spend time contacting everyone after auditions to tell them yes or no. The cruellest thing is to be left in limbo after you have given what you feel is a good audition.

These audition speeches give both sides of the argument as to whether it really was a good idea to leave everything behind and start a new life in America.

- Kate Glover,
writer, *Mayflower*

AUDITION MONOLOGUE A

Elizabeth Winslow was the wife of the celebrated Edward Winslow. In the play she is feisty and intelligent and not afraid of expressing her views. So, when asked by Pastor Robinson why she is not keen on going to the New World, this is what she says:

*****

ELIZABETH: I think it is mad. We are able to worship in the way we wish here in Leiden. We are not at risk of being excommunicated or executed - unless we draw attention to ourselves as Elder Brewster and Edward have done. We have no idea what awaits us there - probably nothing at all. Just vast expanses of nothingness. And that would be the best we could expect. At worst, we would be pursued and killed by savage tribes who feel that we are taking away land that isn't ours. I think we should give thanks for the freedom of worship we have here and just stop drawing attention to ourselves.

AUDITION MONOLOGUE B

In 1630, ten years after the arrival of The Mayflower, Bradford wrote the famous 'Of Plymouth Plantation'. He records for posterity the harshness of a seemingly inhospitable continent. Many Americans know this passage well.

*****

BRADFORD: They had no friends to welcome them nor inns to entertain or refresh their weather-beaten bodies; no houses or much less towns to repair to, to seek for succour ... What could now sustain them, but the spirit of God and His Grace? May not and ought not the children of these fathers rightly say: Our fathers were Englishmen which came over this great ocean, and were ready to perish in this wilderness, but they cried unto the Lord, and He heard their voice and looked on their adversity.

THE GIRL WHO JUMPED OFF
THE HOLYWOOD SIGN
by Joanne Hartstone

(*ISBN 978-0993197581*)

"After all... who would want to look at
Evie Edwards at the fade out?"

An aspiring actress clutches the sides of the Hollywood sign, looking out over the lights of Los Angeles, and the studio system that produced her nightmare. It is 1949: Truman is President, Norma Jean Baker is a little-known model who poses nude for an art calendar in order to recover her impounded car, and nobody has ever heard of Evie Edwards...

Charting a nostalgic journey through the Golden Age of Hollywood, including stories from the Silent Era, the Great Depression and World War II, **JOANNE HARTSTONE**'s play with music for one performer makes a poignant statement about the human cost of America's dream factory, told from a fresh and dark perspective.

"It's a tale we've heard a hundred times before – of broken dreams and shattered lives. But not like this. Not with such emotional truth; not with a roller-coaster ride of feelings, rising to the crest of hopeful possibility and plummeting to the depths of reality, rolling along the rails of innocence into the pit of naivety, only to pick oneself up and resume the steep climb towards the impossible star."

- Peter Wilkins, *Canberra Critics Circle*

Also published by 49Knights

AGAPI MOU
by Donald Horn

(ISBN 978-199365813)

Agapi Mou (which means 'my beloved' in Greek) is part love story, heartache, and historical fiction. This novel engages the reader with five different stories that by the final pages brings together lost lovers whom fifty-seven years earlier were torn apart because of a devastating earthquake. By fate, they are united on a veranda overlooking the Ionian Sea and get to express their love once more. *Agapi Mou* is a moving tribute to the human heart and to survivin the loss of love.

Throughout the pages, you will learn of the history of this small island nestled in the Ionian Sea, which is between Italy and Greece as well as you will meet five very different people that all have a story to tell about their beloved island, Zakynthos.

DONALD HORN has written, directed, and produced over 235 theatrical productions over the course of more than three decade. He is the founder of Triangle Productions based in Portland, Oregon. His first novel, *Crumbs of Love and That's All You Get*, was published in 2006.

The Greek language edition of *Agapi Mou* (ISBN 9781-999365820) is also published by 49Knights.

THE LUCK OF THE DEVIL
by David Damant

(*ISBN 978-0993197550*)

"The club's nonpareil dramaturge."

- Rupert Hill, March 2016

Vienna, May 1931. The Baron Bretzenny is a worried man.
His banking house is bust. It seems nothing can prevent
the Bank Bretzenny from becoming just another casualty,
lost amid the global wreckage of the Wall Street Crash. As
one of Vienna's foremost public atheists, the Baron literally
hasn't got a prayer.

Then a mysterious visitor offers the Baron a way out of his
troubles... but at what price?

The Luck of the Devil is the coruscating debut comedy of
financial guru turned scribbler, **DAVID DAMANT**.

Damant was at once both a respected elder statesman in the
realm of finance, a pioneer of Modern Portfolio Theory in
Europe, and also a keen observer of his fellow creatures,
their vanities and profanities.

The Luck of the Devil presents readers with beautifully
observed characters, set in sparkling dialogue, with
sufficient authenticity to delight both kings in their
counting houses and struggling artists in their drafty
garrets.

Also published by 49Knights

ANTIGONE ALONE: A PLAY
FOR ONE WOMAN
by Michael McEvoy

(ISBN 978-0993197574)

The story of Oedipus' accidental marriage to his own mother, the discovery of and fallout from their unintended incest, is among the most recognisable from the classical Greek legacy.

> "Antigone Alone will make a great one-woman show. It reads really well, with good humour early on. It's clear, intelligent, vivid, witty and tragic."

> - Dr David Bellingham, Programme Director, MA Art Business, Sotheby's Institute of Art, London.

The remarkable achievement of this lastest incarnation of an auld classic, is to have reawakened Antigone in a more human-scale context where the drama, tragedy, and even comedy of her predicament can shine through, devoid of operatic embellishment. The result is as sharp as a hoplite's spear, as swift as trireme under sail, as monstrous and as savage as a cyclops taking his three-headed hellhound out for a walk.

On television **MICHAEL McEVOY** was, for some reason, most likely to be seen appearing as a member of the legal profession: as a magistrate in the BBC comedy series *Chambers*, as defence solicitors in several episodes of *The Bill*, as well as in *Trail of Guilt – Who Cared for Billie-Jo?* Michael was unsure whether his role as a prosecution barrister in the BBC's *Watching the Detectives* counted as a promotion or a demotion.

Also published by 49Knights

NO SMALL THING
by VERONICA HANDOVER

(ISBN 978-1999365806)

All of a sudden, Carla's life is turned upside down by a secret from her husband's past. Has their long marriage been broken by betrayal? Is the life they share nothing but a sham?

Watching from the sidelines, desperate for the things she never had, the mysterious Rose must weigh her options and possibly confront the total rejection that is her ultimate fear.

Rob, a recently retired architect, pours his energy into the remodeling of his new London house, seemingly unaware that the threads of his home life are unraveling around him.

VERONICA HANDOVER was born in Egypt, where her father was a successful cotton trader. As a young girl, she moved with her family to Peru, before they ultimately settled in Sudan. Veronica completed her schooling in England before going on to study Modern Languages at Cardiff University.

Having achieved a Cambridge Certificate of Education, she taught for a number of years at schools in Swindon where her husband, Richard, was then based. Veronica went on to set up her own nursery pre-school, which she ran for nine years. During that time she moonlighted as an Ofsted inspector and later became an NVQ assessor in Early Years Education. Veronica and Richard have three adult children and divide their time between Wiltshire and the Greek island of Zakynthos.

Also published by 49Knights

SHAKESPEARE, HIS WIFE, AND THE DOG
by Philip Whitchurch

(*ISBN 978-0993197543*)

April 1616. Shakespeare has returned to Stratford a rich famous and successful man but all's not well. Why is he so unhappy? Why can't he sleep? Why is his wife furious with him? Who is Will waiting for and why can't Anne find the dog? The secrets, lies, resentments and passions of a marriage laid bare. A sleepless night in Stratford, the one hour traffic of our play.

"A Bardian trainspotter's delight... this is a script which will belong to the ages" - *FringeReview*

"A joyous celebration of Language." - *The List*

PHILIP WHITCHURCH is an actor, director and writer. His film credits include The English Patient, Blue Ice, Wondrous Oblivion as well as Beowulf and Grendel.

Philip is well known to TV audiences as *The Bill's* Chief Inspector Philip Cato, Captain William Frederickson in *Sharpe*, and the neighbour, Tyler, in *My Hero*. From 1987 he narrated the children's television classic *The Shoe People*.

His West End credits include: The Inspector in *An Inspector Calls*, *The Changing Room*, *Ghost Stories* and the Dad in the musical *Billy Elliot*, a role he reprised on Broadway. Philip has also worked at the National Theatre, The Globe and the Royal Shakespeare Company.

49KNIGHTS
ABOUT US

49Knights was established to do for play scripts what the fair trade movement has done for tea and coffee - to reduce the distance between the producer and the consumer so as to bring maximum reward to the producer and and maximum quality to the consumer. The artists we collaborate with retain 100% ownership of their work and the performance rights. Getting published with 49Knights empowers writers to reach new audiences both in print and on stage.

Our approach to content is inspired by Ben Jonson's 1616 Folio. Jonson was the first English playwright to edit his plays to be read as well as performed. Jonson hoped, as we do, that the result would be as immersive an experience as seeing the scripts performed live. As publishers, our job is to be the studio sound engineer, getting the artist on record with a minimum of distortion and distraction. It's vital to the integrity of each project that the artist makes all the artistic decisions - it's their voice that matters.

This script is published by 49Knights

BROWSE OUR TITLES

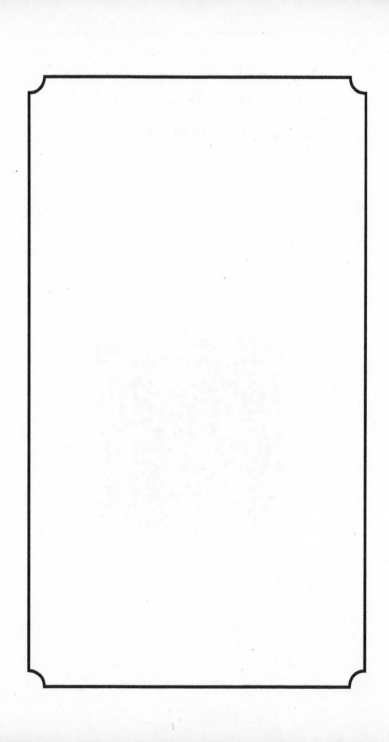